TRANSFORMATION

Coming to Know Jesus and Your Servant Heart

STAN RYNOTT , M.A., LSCW, COG

Love is the primal instinct of your servant heart.

WESTBOW
PRESS®
A DIVISION OF THOMAS NELSON
& ZONDERVAN

WestBow Press books may be ordered through booksellers or by contacting:

WestBow Press
A Division of Thomas Nelson & Zondervan
1663 Liberty Drive
Bloomington, IN 47403
www.westbowpress.com
844-714-3454

Because of the dynamic nature of the Internet, any web addresses or
links contained in this book may have changed since publication and
may no longer be valid. The views expressed in this work are solely those
of the author and do not necessarily reflect the views of the publisher,
and the publisher hereby disclaims any responsibility for them.

Any people depicted in stock imagery provided by Getty Images are
models, and such images are being used for illustrative purposes only.
Certain stock imagery © Getty Images.

ISBN: 979-8-3850-2110-9 (sc)
ISBN: 979-8-3850-2361-5 (hc)
ISBN: 979-8-3850-2111-6 (e)

Library of Congress Control Number: 2024905317

Print information available on the last page.

WestBow Press rev. date: 6/4/2024

If you picked up this book to inspect the table of contents or this dust jacket, you have the curiosity of a person with a yearning soul and likely Servant Heart. You may be ready for Transformation in the discovery of the best possible version of YOU; coming to know God, in breaking the chains of addiction to harmful substances, bad attitudes, dysfunctional behaviors , toxic relationships and in discovering your true purpose in life and making a difference in this chaotic world.

Jeremiah 29:11-14 "For I know the plans I have for you declares the Lord. Plans to prosper you and not harm you. Plans to give you hope and a future." I was raised in church but I was not tuned in. God says love God, love people. Mom said God is LOVE and so does Jesus. I didn't get it. I was an angry boy and a ticked off teen. It got me nowhere.

I was shy, quiet and socially awkward. The bullies zoomed in. I felt bad about myself and retreated. My solace was in music. The music of our youth is what we relate to when all else seems lost. The songs we grow up with are the chorus of our lives. Then a Bob Dylan song told me "ya gotta serve somebody." I thought to myself "What are you talking about Bob, You want me to be a waiter? Mad again. No more church.

In March of 2017 I accepted an invitation to service at Our Saviors Church. The worship music lit my pilot light and the Pastor lit my fire. I raised my hands and Jesus saved me from me. New Life is a process of growing Peace, Contentment and Purpose. Self discipline is self love. Transformation begins with loving yourself as Jesus loves us. Unconditionally. Thanks for caring.

CONTENTS

Section 4. The Gospels of Matthew, Mark, Luke and John / Epistles, People, Places and Parables. Signs and wonders. Love, hope and peace.

Section 5. The Apostles, the Early Christians, and the Holy Spirit Carry on.

Section 6. The Pauline Epistles (13 letters). From Epiphany to Purpose

Section 7. The Post Pauline Epistles and John's Revelation

ACKNOWLEDGEMENTS

First and foremost, I am humbled in thankfulness gratitude and reverence for God, my holy Father and Jesus Christ, who is my savior, teacher, and guiding light. Also, the Holy Spirit of comfort, help and intercession, who is our advocate before God and the Holy Spirit of truth.

I give special thanks for my mother, Donna Jean Darting-Rynott, who lived a life worthy of her calling to nurture and comfort her bratty boys, and so many others, with the Kingdom of Heaven truth of "God is love-God is love - God is Love."

I give thanks to my dad; my father of earth, Stanley Thomas Rynott; who gave us the discipline, attention, and the work ethic to succeed in life.

Also, where would our parents have been without grandparents, aunts, uncles, older cousins, friends, and neighbors to contribute to the safety, guidance, and maturation of the little *"puddle jumping schemers."* Sadly, all but the cousins are gone now. Families are truly the bread of life in God's kitchen, and we give thanks for our daily bread.

I never knew my paternal grandfather (also with no middle name). He only knows me from heaven. But still, I want to mention my namesake who passed away during a simple surgical procedure before I was born.

Dad had just got on the boat for the Korean War with his Browning automatic rifle. Machine gunners are prime targets on the battlefield. The Red Cross flew him home for the "original" Stanley Rynott's funeral service.

Fortunately, dad missed that boat. When his home time was up, an officer who knew he had some college education changed his MOS (Military Occupational Specialty), to Quartermaster. Quartermasters supply and support the frontline soldiers. I cannot help but wonder if the first Stanley saved his two successors. See you soon Grandpa!

I am also thankful to my typist, Holly, who was very supportive and patient with my I T struggles, and my new friend Cully whose expertise in photo editing and copyright procedure was an invaluable blessing to this project.

And last, but certainly not least, I want to give thanks, gratitude, and heartfelt appreciation for all my Pastors, church leaders, church professional staff, volunteers, mentors, and small group friends who have poured into me, since the first day of the rest of my life, when I was delivered in Our Savior's Church, March of 2017.

SECTION 1

Introduction to Transformation / Old Testament Creation – New Testament Truth

---

Genesis means beginning or origin. This is the story of creation and God's purpose and plans for us. The Bible is the book of beginnings that ends in Revelation. Creation is formation. We are all formed in our mother's womb, in just a wink of time in the father's eye.

Recent research at Northwestern University has detected a microscopic flash of light at the instant of conception.

Genesis 1: In the beginning God created the heavens and the earth.

Genesis 1:26: "Then God said, *'let us make mankind in OUR image, in OUR likeness, so that they may rule over the fish of the sea, and the birds of the sky, all the livestock, and all the wild animals, and all the creatures that move along the ground.'"*

Formation is the beginning of Transformation.

The Word Became Flesh

John 1: 1 *"In the beginning was the Word, and the Word was with God, and the word was God."*

John 1: 4-5 *"In him was life, and that life was the Light of all mankind. The Light shines in the darkness, and the darkness has not overcome it"*

John 1: 14 *"Word became flesh, it made his dwelling among us. We have seen his glory, the glory of the one and only son, who came from the Father, full of grace and truth."*

When we become deliberate Christians, our Transformation begins. To be a deliberate Christian means to walk in the word of God with boldness, and regularity. When we have the supernatural revelation of grace and truth, we humans naturally want to pay it forward. We want to increase the Kingdom.

From Pastor Scott Adam's book, **The Discipleship Book.** *"Success is not what you pursue, it is who you attract by the person you become."*

Jesus does not call the qualified, he qualifies the called. A disciple is someone who follows, learns from, and imitates Jesus.

Lead by example. When we obey God's word; we receive grace and pay if forward. Amazing Grace is the gift that keeps on giving.

Our Savior's Church core values are "Come to know God, find freedom, discover your purpose and make a difference."

John 14:12 *"Very truly, I tell you, whoever believes in me will do the works I have done, and they will do even greater things, because I am going back to the Father."*

John 14:14 *"And I will do whatever you ask in my name."*

Ordinary Men- Idiotas

In Luke 9, Jesus calls the twelve disciples altogether. He gave them the power and authority to drive out all demons, cure all diseases and to proclaim the Kingdom of God.

In John 16, Jesus told his disciples he was going away. *"Unless I go away, the advocate will not come to you. When he comes, he will prove the world to be in the wrong about sin, righteousness, and judgement."*

Jesus was crucified, rose from the dead and appeared to his disciples ten times. He came to continue to encourage and empower them.

Acts 2 In Jerusalem

Fifty days after the Passover celebration of liberation from Egyptian slavery, the disciples attended the Festival of Weeks, or Shavuot, which was an international event, also known as the Pentecost. On that occasion, the Holy Spirit fell on the disciples and three thousand believers in Christ!

Acts 2:2 *"Suddenly, a sound like a blowing of a violent wind, came from heaven."*

Acts 2:4 *"They were filled with the Holy Spirit and began to speak in tongues."*

Acts 2:6 *"Each one heard their own language."*

Acts 3:1 After this, Peter and John were BOLD in addressing the crowds, especially with a man who had been lame since birth, and then begging at the gate of the temple. (The Gate's name was "Beautiful").

And Peter spoke to him, *"Gold and silver we do not have, but this I will give you. In the name of Jesus, walk!"* The man instantly got up. He walked and jumped around the temple.

And the members of the council were amazed at the boldness of these men, who they recognized as followers of Jesus, and ordinary men. (In Greek "**Idiotas**").

Who were these Idiotas to challenge their authority? How brazen, how BOLD! (In Greek *"Parrhesia"*).

Eventually, all the disciples, except John were killed for their boldness. *"Being bold means letting God lead you."* Paster Scott Adams.

We all have a TRANSFORMATION story, a testimony to share and encourage others to share theirs. For we are all a work in progress.

The Gospel of the Kingdom by George Elden Ladd reads; *"The Kingdom of God came to earth in human form 2023 years ago and man could reject it."* (And they did. And we do).

From his Roman prison cell, even John the Baptist; Jesus's cousin, began to doubt. So he sent envoys to seek Jesus out and inquire. Was he really the promised one?

When found, Jesus replied that he was indeed the bearer of the Kingdom, that the signs of the Messianic age of prophecy were being manifested, and yet Jesus said, *"Blessed is he who takes no offense at me."* (He knew that was coming at him).

"Yes, the Kingdom of God is here. But there is a mystery, a new revelation about the Kingdom. It is here, but instead of destroying human sovereignty, it attacked the sovereignty of Satan." (And most importantly). Instead of making changes in the external political order of things, Jesus is making changes in the spiritual order in the lives of men and women."

So, what does this mean? It is up to us, individually and collectively, to change the world, one soul at a time. We do not need to be an ordained minister, pastor, or priest, if we walk with our servant heart. God is love.

1 Corinthians 13:13 *"And now these three remain: Faith, Hope and Love. But the greatest of these is love."*

The Greatest Commandment

Matthew 22:34 The Pharisees (experts in mosaic law), together to test Jesus and inquired (with fake regard), teacher, *"which is the greatest commandment in the law?"*

Matthew 22:37 Jesus replied, *"love the Lord your God, with all your heart and with all your soul and with all you mind."*

Matthew 22:38 *"This is the first and greatest commandment."*

Matthew 22:39 And the second is like it, *"love your neighbor as yourself."*

Matthew 22:40 *"All the law and prophets hang on these two commandments."*

*"**The love language minute,**"* by Gary Chapman

"Love begins with an attitude" (honor- from his book The 5 Love Languages); which in turn leads to acts of service.

Psalm 8:5 (King David*)*, *"You have made them a little lower than the angels and crowned them with glory and honor."*

Psalm 8:6 *"You made them rulers over the works of your hands.* Mom *"God is love. God is love. God is love."*

The Apostle of Love

The Apostle Paul was and still is the greatest encourager. He sets the human bar for acts of love, only second to Jesus. As Saul the Pharisee, he persecuted and killed the early Christians that he saw as blasphemers.

Saul hit the ultimate bottom as a drunkard of power on the road to Damascus when the voice of Jesus brought him to his knees and changed his life. He became the greatest proponent of the love of Jesus. Paul went on to write more than half the books of the New Testament.

The best way we can honor God the Father, Jesus and the Holy Spirit who dwells in us, is to begin to live and walk in the way of LOVE, which is seen in our ever developing compassionate, and uplifting servant hearts.

How many of you know the uplifting and encouraging nature of our pastors, ministers, and priests is infectious?

Philippians 4:5 Paul proclaimed *"Rejoice in the Lord, I say again rejoice! Let your gentleness be evident to all who would see!"*

Matthew 5:16 *"In the same way let your light shine before others, that they may see your good deeds and glorify your Father in heaven."*

(play *"Love God, Love People,"* by Danny Gokey).

This will be the first of dozens of worship music video suggestions that I believe are like seasonings sprinkled on and complimentary to the scripture and sentiment of the text. I pray that these songs will be as encouraging and empowering as they were to me on my first day as a deliberate Christian at the age of 63 in March of 2017.

In Pastor Craig Groeschel's daily devotional, Daily Power for March 1st, he describes how Satan uses social media and cultural pressure (trivial differences and petty competitions) to divide us. He says, *"In order to grow in our faith, we must stand out in the right ways at the right time for the right reasons to change the direction of our lives."* So let us have discernment and desire based on the love of God to change the direction of our lives and get into the habit of encouraging others and lift the spiritually suppressed and immature in faith. God loves us too much to leave us where we are.

This book is for people who may have grown accustomed to the convenience of streaming Sunday service and are herein reminded of the power of the Holy Spirit presence in the Church sanctuary that resonates in the Body of Christ (Us) but dulled from the pulpit of a tv box.

It is for the passively curious, the agnostic and, hopefully, prayerfully for the atheist more in need of faith than he or she knows.

It is for people who may have been, or still are, as lost or complaent as I was when I quit the church after leaving college and my family to get a job and get married to my future ex-wife.

It is also for those standing at or down the street from the door of spiritual revival and fulfillment in Jesus Christ. Matthew 7:7 Ask, Seek, Knock: "Ask and it will be given to you; Seek and ye shall find; knock and the door will be opened to you."

God is not the tyrant in this world. He created us as creatures with free will, so that the righteous choices we make will be out of love for Jesus and others. Self-discipline is self-love. God is love. Jesus is God on earth. A divine hand to shake with the heart of service to embrace.

Philippians 4:6-7: "*Do not be anxious in anything, but in every situation, by prayer and petition; with thanksgiving, present your request to God. And the peace which transcends all understanding will guard your hearts and minds in Jesus Christ.*"

The compassion of Christ overcame the world. He is the light, and in his light, we become deliberate and intentional in our vision and purpose on earth.

Paul accepted by the Apostles.

In Galatians 2 Saul the Pharisee; conformed in the strictest manner to the laws of Moses and legalistic priestly code. The Pharisees and other religious leaders believed in the coming of the Messiah and expected a deliverer from their Roman oppressors but rejected Jesus and flaunted their authority over others while not genuinely righteous in their hard hearts. Saul oversaw the stoning of Stephan when he called them out on their blatant hypocrisy. In Galatians 2:19-21 Paul explains, "*For through the law I died to the law so that I might live for God. I have been crucified with Christ and I no longer live, but Christ lives in me. The life I now live in the body, I live by faith in the son of man, who loved me and gave himself to me. I do not* set aside the grace of God, for if righteousness could be gained through the law, Christ died for nothing."

No Greater Love

John 15:13 *"Greater love has no one than this: to lay down one's life for one's friends."*

John 3:16 *"For God so loved the world, that he gave his only son, that whoever believes in him shall not perish, but have eternal life."*

(play song *"God So Loved"* by We the Kingdom).

We do not have to die to discover and live our servant heart, but as we grow in our faith, and calling to serve, the old parts of ourselves, our bad instincts, attitudes and habits of selfishness, abusiveness, neglect, and insecurities slowly but surely die out of us. Ordinary people can boldly walk out into this world in the confidence of our convictions. Parrhesia Idiotas arise!

"For Whom the Bell Tolls," by John Donne:

"No man is an island entire of itself. Every man is a piece of continent, a part of the main. If clod be washed away by sea, our country is the less for it. Just as any promontory or manner of thy friend, or theine own were. For you see, the death of any man, diminishes me because I am involved in mankind. Therefore, never send to know, for who the bell tolls. It tolls for thee."

In Philippians 2:1-4 The Apostle Paul proclaimed; *"therefore if you have any encouragement from being united with Christ, if any comfort from his love, if any common sharing, if any tenderness, and compassion, then make my joy complete by being likeminded, having he same love, being one in the spirit and of one mind.* In humility value others above yourselves."

So, my hope for you is that this book, which is about TRANSFORMATION, will be a fruitful journey because life IS a journey. The great philosopher, Forrest Gump famously said "*Life is like a box of chocolates, you never know what you are going to ge-et.*"

My disappointment was in the candy with coconut. Not that it tasted bad, it was just the texture that bugged me. Our box of chocolates is people, places, and things. In my TRANSFORMATION, coconut became good to me. Revelation. The coconut is a "chocolate delivery system!" Life is hard, Jesus is goodness! Jesus reminds us that love is the primal instinct of our servant heart and we all have our own coconut to get over.

CHAPTER 1

Worship Music (Humility, Indivisible, Fellowship and Revelation)

Humility. Indivisible. Fellowship. Revelation.

After I left my parents in 1975, church attendance consisted of weddings, funerals, and every other Christmas Eve with my family in Illinois.

I had seen some images and videos of worship music in church services, with the worship team "rock band" configurations, who were belting out the Holy Spirit in song and adoration. But the Holy Spirit is not as strong in a tv box as it was in person on the first day of the rest of my life (March 2017), as a newly formed and deliberate Christian at Our Saviors Church in Broussard, LA.

That worship music revealed to me what I had been ignorant of for sixty-three years! I used to think that I just needed to treat people like God wants us to. Worship? It was in a song that Bob Dylan told me; "Ya gotta serve somebody." What? What are you talking about Bob? Do you want me to be a waiter? I was clueless. (Un blissful ignorance)

But I got my big clue that day in 2017. Worship keeps us humble and brings us closer to God, Jesus, and the Holy Spirit inside us. Daughter, sister, spouse and son; stranger, friend and everyone. (See Philippians 2-3).

James 4:6 But he that giveth me grace wherefor he said, *"God resists the proud, but he gives grace to the humble."*

I was prideful. My wife referred to me as "Cowboy." I did not know how to listen to her or the Holy Spirit inside me.

Luke 18:4 *"For all those who exult themselves will be humbled and those who are humbled, will be exalted."* Saul, the killer, became Paul, the Apostle of Love, on the road to Damascus.

Humility

Philippians 2 Imitating Christ

Philippians 2:6 *"Christ, who being in the very nature of God, did not consider equality with God something to be used to his own advantage, rather he made himself nothing by taking the very nature of a servant, being made in human likeness."*

Humility is a blessing. Humility brings grace and forgiveness: for yourself and others, and peace...abundantly!

PEACE: A mentality of tranquility built upon a relationship with the Holy Spirit of humility,

Above small differences and petty competitions.

A new way of life walking in Grace with Harmony, Serenity, Security, Confidence, Contentment, and a divine sense of Wellbeing. Walking in Amazing Grace.

Amazing Grace: the gift that keeps on giving!

We pay it forward with our servant hearts.

> play "*Peace on Earth*," by Austin French/ official lyrics video).

The Holy Bible contains 177 verses on humility. We are all a work in progress.

For you God, I give my thanks! Your word, your wisdom, and your Son.
Above you Lord, there is not one.
At sixty-three, I had no clue. At O S C; I then found you.
Your Word is Gold, your Love is True
My cowboy ways are mostly through.
A better husband, and a man.
To the deceiver, be you damned.
No shame, no fear as I draw near.
Though perfect not, you hold me dear. AMEN

The book of Psalms is a book of divine poetry for the expression of praise, worship, and confession to God. Seventy-five are from the heart of King David, Asaph wrote twelve; the descendants of Korah wrote eleven and Solomon wrote two.

The Psalms are SONGS of praise to God as our creator, sustainer, and redeemer. Praise is recognizing, appreciating, and expressing God's greatness. They help us focus our thoughts on God's mercy. They move us to praise him and make ourselves better.

The Psalms are trials and tribulations; our failures that lead to success. They are a microcosm of good, the bad and the ugly of human nature; juxtaposed with and redeemed in the overcoming beauty in a song of the heavenly trio.

Psalms twenty-three, a psalm of David, *"The Lord is my shepherd, I lack nothing. He makes me lie down in green pastures, he leads me besides still waters, he refreshes my soul, he guides me along the right path, for his name's sake. Even though I walk through the darkest of valleys, I will fear no evil, for you are with me, your rod, your staff, they comfort me."*

(play, *"Nobody,"* by Casting Crowns with Matthew West).

Humility, Prayer, and Worship is music to God's ears.

This book will be seasoned with Christian worship music video suggestions to tune into in that moment, to enhance the text and light the path of your servant heart journey. Also, worship is merely your humble means of expressing gratitude to the Father, the Son, and the Holly Spirit.

Note: What works best is to google search "Play song_____by_____" __.

Enjoy and soothe your servant heart. You deserve it! God loves you. I do not know you, the reader, but God knows you by name, who you are and where you have been.

Thank you for joining us on this journey. As I write this line, I do not yet know what scripture, sentiment, song, message, or insight that I will attempt to deliver from this constructive collaboration and confluence of the Old Testament, and each book of Jesus' New Testament.

We were made to be re-made, brand new creations. As we study and grow together, I hope you will feel the peace and spirit of fellowship in Jesus. You may even feel moved to share something of your journey with others on the walk of Children of God.

"Nothing is simple and alone. The breathing mountains, the living stones, each blade of grass, the clouds, the rain, each star, the beasts, the birds, and the invisible spirits of the air- we are all one, indivisible. Nothing that any of us does but affects us all." From "The Man Who Killed the Deer," by Frank Waters. A short story in *"Seasons of Light in Atchafalaya Basin,"* by Greg Guirard.

"He Prayuth well who loveth well, both man and bird and beast. He Prayuth best who loveth best, all things great and small; for the dear God who loveth us. He made and loveth all.," by Samuel Tyler Coleridge.

Job 12:29 *"But ask now the beasts, and they shall teach thee; and the fowls of the air, and they shall tell thee. Or speak to the earth, and it shall teach thee; and the fishes of the sea shall declare unto thee; that the hand of the Lord hath wrought this."*

God created all creatures, great and small, and we can indeed learn from nature and even about love from the beasts of the wild.

A few years ago, I watched a documentary about baby animals in Africa that had been orphaned by poachers and saved by the humans of a wild animal rescue organization. Each baby was assigned a single human caregiver. They were fed and cared for and eventually trained for life back in the jungle; to be reunited with their respective animal families. One of the care givers got curious. What would happen if they came upon their grown-up orphans in the wild?

It Took a Leap of Faith.

In each case, there was a warm and tender embrace. And then departure back into the trees and a hint of sadness from the human and a pregnant pause. And then the re-emergence, only this time with the animals and their entire families! No fear, no worries, just love and hugs and play. The new babies were all over their human aunts and uncles. You cannot tell me there is not a universal spirit of love! Some of us are in for a massive surprise. A revelation or even an epiphany.

"Hi, my name is Stan. On this twenty second day of January 2023, and this is the first day of the rest of your life."

Shalom-Peace!

Can we just pray for a new dawn of daily blessings? Let us try a worship song together and see how it fits.

> (play, *"Joy in the Morning,"* by, Taurin Wells) ….and
> now we praise and celebrate Jesus Christ!

The Greatest Man in History

He had no servants, yet they called him Master.
He had no degrees; yet they called him a teacher.
He had no medicines, yet they called him a healer.
He had no army, yet kings feared him.
He won no military battles, yet he conquered the world.
He committed no crimes, yet they crucified him.
He split time and history by his very presence on earth.
And he came with grace to save us, to rescue all who would care to call his name.

CHAPTER 2

The Search

Love and Service from the books of the Bible and other writings inspired by the God of Love, the Prince of Peace, and the Holy Spirit of truth.

We will continue to explore inspiring knowledge and wisdom from authors of some of the thousands of books of prose, poetry and quotes based on the love and direction from the "The Good Book."

We will notice a flow of reoccurring themes, sentiments, wisdoms, teachings, directions, and warnings throughout both the Testaments of the Bible. We will read examples of messages from secular authors who have been inspired and driven to share God's love and promote the Kingdom of God and the servant heart.

There is a four-hundred-year gap between Malachi, at the end of the Old Testament, and the Book of Matthew in the New Testament.

The book of Matthew is the first New Testament telling of the greatest story ever told. The life and lesson of our Lord, Savior and teacher, Jesus Christ who loved us enough to transition from one certainty to another. From Heaven in his Father's House to Hades on Earth that he accepted as his path to lead us on our path of redemption, renewal, and everlasting life. Jesus showed us how to live, love, lead others, and to walk with him in the fellowship of the Servant King.

K-Love on Demand

Before we dig in, I would like to recommend another worship song and radio station. Positive Encouraging K-Love Radio is a contemporary Christian music station that has an American and Global presence. I enthusiastically recommend a regular turn in to the station and a download of the **K-Love on Demand App** for positive and encouraging music, original content, concerts, and jam sessions from Red Rocks Park and Amphitheater to the intimate settings like Brandon Heath's back yard and with Andrew Ripp at the historic Koinonia Bookstore and Coffeehouse on music row in Nashville, TN.

I also have the K-Love Radio Station App and recommend the K-Love Challenge to see how thirty days of focus on positive and encouraging music can effect your mood and outlook on life. I personally have been on this challenge since I began writing to you on January 15, 2023.

Oh! I just thought about another song. Love Train (can you find it?)

For now, and before we open to the next section of your journey, I recommend you all tune in to Danny Gokey; and see how *Tell your Heart to Beat Again*" touches you.

SECTION 2

Love and Service in the Old Testament / The promise of the messiah and salvation

CHAPTER 1

The Consistency of God's love

The Old Testament contains the first two concepts of the Bible:

1) The creation 2) The fall of man

I recall going through the Old Testament for the first time and reading the portions and verses recommended by our Pastors.

In the Old Testament, God may seem very different before the arrival of Jesus who came with a New Testament and a new covenant with his children. Even though our Father can be stern and even harsh in rebuilding his children or even in the destruction of evil nations, God is now, and always will be in charge. More importantly, God is eternal love. The prophet Isaiah speaks to us in the eternal nature of God's love for us.

Isaiah 54:10 "Though the mountains be shaken, and the hills be removed, yet my unfailing love for you will not be shaken."

(play *"Same God,"* by Elevation Worship).

Romans 5:8-9 "But God demonstrates his own love for us in this; while we were still sinners, Christ died for us." This reminds us of God's enduring love for us.

Jesus Christ knew his fate among humans, and more importantly, his mission on earth, which was to die for our sins, for our sanctification, (to be set apart from sin) and justified, (as if we had never sinned.) We are to understand the eternal love of, and in, the Kingdom of God and then join him and others as co-inheritors of God's Kingdom.

Isaiah 53 is traditionally understood to speak of Jesus as the coming Messiah and as a Prophecy for us; uniquely divine in that he came to love, teach, inspire, motivate guide, and direct us on a path illuminated by his eternal flame. Before and after his ultimate sacrifice.

Isaiah 53:5 *"But he was persecuted for our transgressions, and he was crushed for our iniquities; the punishment that brought us peace was on him, and by his wounds we are healed."*

No Greater Love is This

John 15:13 *"To lay down one's life that others may live."* (Literally and in spiritual renewal).

1 Samuel 12:24 *"But be sure to fear the Lord and serve him faithfully with all your heart, consider what great things he has done for you."*

Nehemiah 9:17 They refused to listen, *"But you are a forgiving God, gracious and compassionate, slow to anger and abounding in steadfast love, so you did not forsake them."*

Proverbs 16:32 *"He who is slow to anger is better than the who conquers a city."*

James 1:19 "Take note, everyone should be quick to listen, slow to speak and slow to become angry, because anger does not produce the righteousness that God desires."

Jeremiah 31:31 *"The days are coming, declares the Lord, when I will make a New Covenant with the people of Israel, and with the people of Judah. It will not be like the Covenant I made with their ancestors when I took them out of Egypt, because they broke my covenant, though I was husband to them,"* declares the Lord.

"I will put my law into their minds and write it on their hearts and I will be their God, and they will be my people. No longer will they teach their neighbor, or say to one another, "know the Lord," because they will all know me from the least of them to the greatest."

And in the Lord, we can be the best possible version of ourselves. Let your servant heart be known to all who would see.

John 14:12 And Jesus told his disciples, and so says to us still, *"truly, truly I tell you who ever believes in me will do the works I have been doing, and greater words they will do because I am going to the Father. And I will do anything you ask in my name, so that the Father may be glorified in the Son."*

The book of Proverbs:

Purpose and Themes from Solomon, the son of David, King of Israel. Instruction for understanding the words of insight, for receiving, instruction in prudent behavior, what is right, just, and fair.

"For giving prudence to those who are simple, knowledge and discretion to the young. Let the wise listen and add to their learning, and let the discerning get guidance for understanding."

Proverbs and parables; the sayings and riddles of the wise:

"The fear of the Lord is the beginning of knowledge, but fools despise wisdom and instruction."

So, help us God, in this broken, angry, and selfish world, to remember that as children of God, and followers of Jesus, we each have a unique purpose, individually and collectively, that is beyond, and different from, human purpose. Help us to see trust and relax in the knowledge and the wisdom you bless us with. You lead us to a purpose beyond our own. And it is in Jesus' name we pray, AMEN.

Romans 8:28 *"And we know that in all things God works for the good of those who love him, who have been called according to his purpose."*

Romans 8:30 *"And those he predestined, he also called, those he called he also justified, those he justified, he also glorified."*

Psalms 100:1-2 *"Shout for joy to the Lord, all the earth, worship the Lord with gladness; come before him with joyful songs. Know that the Lord is God."*

> (play *"Joy to the World"* by English Minister, Isaac Watts, 1719).

In the last book of the Old Testament, Malachi the author recognizes brokenness, willful disobedience, and disrespect, even in Jerusalem. They followed their gods. They were unrighteous and self-serving. God's chosen rejected him, but faith, hope and love were still possible because of God's unfailing love for us, in the promised Messiah, our Savior, Redeemer, teacher and our guiding light.

The book of Malachi is tense and fierce but salted with hope in admonitions and glad prophecy.

> (play *"Living Hope"* by Phil Wickham).

Malachi 4:2 *"But for you who revere my name, the Son of Righteousness will rise with healing in its wings. And you will go out and frolic like well-fed calves."*

This is the Gospel, the Good News of the Kingdom of God. No matter how many times God's children fall from grace; God finds a way to bring us back to unite in our servant hearts. We are reminded that God's love is supernatural, unfailing, faithful, and full of hope in the relationships we find in the Father, the Son, the Holy Spirit.

And Jesus went off to pray in private. John 17:20-23 *"That all of them be one Father."* (To the Holy Father) *"just as you are in me, and I am in you, may they also be in us, joined together in complete unity so that the world may believe that you have sent me; so that they may be brought to complete unity."*

CHAPTER 2

The Consistency between the Old and New Testaments

Leviticus 19:18 "Don't seek revenge or bear a grudge against anyone among your people but love your neighbor as yourself. I am the Lord."

1 John 4:7-9 "Dear friends, let us love one another for love comes from God. Everyone who loves, has been born of God and knows God. Whoever does not love, does not know God because GOD IS LOVE. This is how God showed his love among us, he sent his one and only son into the world that we might live through him."

1 Corinthians 13:13 "Son now these three remain; faith, hope and love; but the greatest of these is love."

> (play *"If I Can Dream"* by Elvis Presley/ Hologram with Celine Dion).

King David says in Psalm 46:1 *"I pray and hope that with the help of God and our own efforts, that we will continue to remain united, because in unity there is strength. God is our refuge, strength, and ever-present help in troubles."*

We are better together

(play *"Amazing Grace,"* by Phil Wickham).

SECTION 3

Love and Service in the New Testament / A New Covenant

A new Covenant Promise

The New Testament contains the last two of four concepts of the Bible.

1) Redemption- to be brought back and restored by God's grace, as if we had never sinned.
   through the sacrifice of Jesus.
2) Restoration- Blessed by a new life, walking in the light of Jesus Christ's love.

CHAPTER 1

The consistency in the fulfillment of Old Testament prophecy

The New Testament is the fulfilment of the Old Testament promise of redemption and restoration through the sacrifice of Jesus Christ. The repetitions, detail, consistency, teachings, and goodness of God between the two of the Testaments; reveals the unfailing nature of God's will, love, desires, and eternal hope for each and all of us culminating in the Grace for God to send his son, to suffer and die for us and welcome us to the Body of Christ, and the Kingdom of God. Grace is undeserved goodwill. A gift from God.

(play *"Amazing Grace My Chains are Broken,"* by Chris Tomlin).

And I thank you God for yet another wonderful day on earth. For all your many blessings and even the hardships and challenges that lead us to you. You lift us up, and we rise above.

And I thank you most for the greatest story ever told; the life and lesson of your Son, Jesus Christ, who died for us on the cross that we might be forgiven our sins, but only by your Grace Father, as we totally put all our trust and dependence on Him for our salvation.

And we thank you Father, for the serenity to accept the circumstances and people that we cannot change, the courage to change what we can, and your wisdom to know the difference.

So, help us Father to not be unwise or unkind as the day's frustrations, failures, disappointments, setbacks, hardships, and vexing people lead us down a path to frustration, anger, offended ness and unforgiveness. Let no unkind thought or word linger in our minds or part our lips as we hear our Holy Spirit, Our Helper, whisper to us, "Be still, for I am with you," (or "Silence," if that is what we need to hear.) And you stop us in our tracks. You lead us back, Father God. You call us back, by your GRACE to the peace of Christ.

Father God, we must not allow the deceiver to steal the joy we have found in you. So, help us Father, to remember, appreciate and participate each day in the ongoing process of yielding to your word, your wisdom, your spirit, and your love.

The ongoing process of developing the character of Jesus Christ; the potential in each of us, revealed and actuated in daily prayer, mediation, and devotionals; as well as in Christian ministry and Christian fellowship, that we deliberately seek.

We dread the notion of falling behind you to embolden the deceiver to our ears. Your word is our shield, Father. Your word is our guard. If we don't let it down, you won't let us down, by your Grace, Father. Your Amazing Grace- the gift that keeps on giving. We pay it forward and deliberately so: walking in your word, your wisdom your love and your Grace; with purpose a means and a method because we are only human. We leak and need refilling. We fall behind you. We get lost.

We have bad instincts and impulses; bad attitudes and negative associations. We fail to count our blessings and miss our appointments with you. Father God, we are sinners and what we seek is your forgiveness and, even more so, to forgive others as you forgive us. You are my Lord and Master I need trust and desire to humbly serve. Humbly serve you and so serve others. Because you show us Father God, that your true Greatness and any genuine goodness in me comes with humility and it is my pride that comes before the fall.

So, Father I know, I understand, I realize acknowledge and confess: Your thoughts are not my thoughts, your words are not my words, and your nature is not my nature; except- as saved by your Grace, it becomes my daily joy and our ultimate destination. And it is in Jesus' holy name I pray AMEN.

Play "Gratitude" (chosen performance) by Brandon Lake

and "Joyful" by Dante Bowe

CHAPTER 2

Gratitude and Thankfulness

Psalm 100:4-4-5 *"Give thanks to him that praise his name for the Lord is good and his love endures forever, his faithfulness continues through all generations."*

Psalm 118 *"This is the day that the Lord has made, we will rejoice and be glad in it."*

Psalm 28:7 *"The Lord is my strength and my shield, my heart trusted in him, and I am helped."*

Psalm 23:1-4 *"The Lord is my Shepard; I shall not want. He makes me lie down in green pasture, he leads me beside quiet waters, he refreshes my soul. He guides me along the right paths for his name's sake. Even though I walk through the valley of death, I will fear no evil, for you are with me. Your rod and your staff; they comfort me. Surely your goodness and love will follow me all the days of my life."*

2 Corinthians 4:15 *"All this for your benefit, so that the Grace that is reaching more and more people may cause Thanksgiving to overflow*

to the Glory of God. Therefore, we don't lose heart…. we are being renewed day by day."

James 1:3 " ..because you know that the testing of your faith produces perseverance."

Romans 5. Peace and Hope: 1 "Therefore, since we have been justified through faith, we have peace with God through our lord Jesus Christ… And we boast in the hope of the glory of God. 3 Not only so, but we also glory in our sufferings, because we know that suffering produces 4 perseverance, perseverance character rand character hope." With the deliberate daily and situational practice of prayer, expressions of gratitude, thankfulness and even reading your 5 favorite affirmations or counting your blessings has a clinically proven benefit on the quality of life. Long term emotional wellness is effected by replacing our cerebral neuro-net's accumulation of negative junk with positive thoughts and attitudes, contentment and even Joy in New Life: Mentally, emotionally and spiritually in The Body of Christ.

CHAPTER 3

Discipleship: Paul's transformation - Our Transformation

The connection between Matthew 28:16-20 and Romans 1:1-3

In the gospel of Matthew, verses 8:16, after the crucifixion and resurrection of Jesus, the remaining disciples came together and went up on the mountain to meet Jesus as instructed by an angel in Matthew 28:5-7.

When they saw Jesus, they fell out and worshipped him, *(but in verse seven, they saw but they STILL had doubt).*

2 Corinthians *5:7* "For we walk by faith not by sight."

Matthew 28:18-19 In the Great Commission, Jesus got their attention and said to them, *"All authority in heaven and on earth has been given to me. Therefore, go out and make disciples of all nations."*

Romans 1:1-3 Paul who had no doubts after his TRANSFORMATION on the road to Damascus, declared boldly that he was an Apostle and set apart for the gospel of God. The gospel of God promised beforehand through his prophets in the Holy scriptures regarding his son.

Small group Bible study is the next step in the maturation of our faith. In my church, we are blessed to be led by a Pastor who is a Bible Scholar, as well as a very affective preacher and teacher of God's word. It is not Pastor's word, or words, as he so often reminds us, but it is the eternal word of God, unvarnished by any human design.

> (play *"Onward Christian Soldiers."* Words by Sabine
> Baring Gould/1865. Music by Author Sullivan/1871.
> This is the standard of the Salvation Army.)

In 2020 our Pastor Scott changed the name of the small groups to Discipleship Groups, because we, as deliberate Christians are in fact the succeeding generations of the original Disciples- The Makers Dozen.

Paster Scott even blessed us with "The Discipleship Book, Next Steps in Our Spiritual Journey." Also referred to as the "Gold Book." A quote he passed along to us states; *"Success is not what you pursue, but it is who you attract by the person you become."*

There is no copyright on God's words, but we must take care to get it right. God's word is a gift we pay forward, not claiming it as our own, but confessing its' wisdom, sentiment, and joy as reliable and eternal.

2 Timothy 3:16 *"All scripture is God- breathed and is useful for teaching, rebuilding, correcting and training in righteousness so that the servant of God may be thoroughly equipped for every good work.* **Question: Is your servant heart speaking to you?**

Colossians 1:10 *"Then the way you will live will always honor and please the Lord, and your lives will produce every kind of good fruit. All the while, you will grow as you learn to know God, being strengthened with all power according to his glorious might, so that you may have great endurance and patience, and giving joyful thanks to the Father who has qualified you to share in the inheritance of his holy people in the Kingdom of light."*

Discipleship is part of TRANSFORMATION that casual Christians embrace when they make their first steps into deliberate Christianity. We are ready for an opportunity to speak the good news of the Father, the Son, and the Holy Spirit, The Holy Trinity of our new life in Jesus.

Grace Received- Promises Delivered

We anticipate each opportunity to speak life into those plodding in the muck and the mire of temptations and depravities of the world. Being strengthened by God, we are not anxious. We do not need to be a pastor or a priest. We do not need to be a great speaker or a bible scholar. *"We have many great pastors, what we need are more Christians,"* Pastor Scott.

Jesus did not Disciple the Pharisees

He did not engage in consultation with the Sanhedrin. Jesus does not call on the qualified, he qualifies the called! DO YOU HEAR? We do not need to be among the powerful religious or political operatives because we are strengthened by the faith and knowledge growing in us. We disciples are mere mortals who follow and learn from and imitate Jesus. We lead by the example of Christ. We receive grace and we pay it forward. We embrace the command and relish the commission.

The first step in fulfilling the prophecies of the covenant of the New Testament, is to love one another as God so loved us. That means even the most un-loveable among us because we do not know the circumstances of people who are disagreeable. But God does and to love God we must love as our default position and assume, as God does, that they/we, are redeemable and capable of inheriting the Gospel of the Kingdom.

The book of Matthew is the first New Testament telling of the greatest story ever told, and that story is punctuated by calls to action as in Matthew 28:16 *"The Great Commission, which one believes is the supernatural and logical transition from the greatest commandment to the love each other as God loves us."*

The disciples were specifically chosen by Jesus from among ordinary citizens to be bold among them, to learn from his teachings and supernatural goodness, and continue his mission on earth.

(play *"Child of Love"* by We the Kingdom").

In Our Transformational Posture

As descendants of the Makers Dozen, in this modern world we do not risk the same perils they accepted. They were systematically persecuted, tortured and executed for daring to irritate the political and religious powers of their day. Let us pray for Christian brothers and sisters till suffering under the descendants of the Pharisees all around the world.

Amongst us all, Paul's TRANSFORMATION was the most dramatic and consequential. In Paul's former life, he was Saul of Tarsus, the prominent and learned Pharisee who persecuted Jesus and his Parrhesia Idiotas because they dared to disrupt the Jewish

Council's confidence in holding on to their power, prestige and unrighteous wealth. Sound familiar?

(play *"Overcomer"* by Mandisa).

Nothing New Under the Sun

The battle between good and evil is generational and a common underlying theme in the stories of humans across our time on earth, (second only to the theme of beauty.) So, we see that ultimately and eventually, even though it seems slow in coming; God always wins us over.

In this world so deeply and intentionally divided, we can connect with the Holy Spirit of the truth and our servant heart. It hits us like a velvet hammer as God reminds us (Psalms 8) that we are made just a little lower that the angels; constructed for the good.

(play, *"For the Good,"* by Riley Clemmons).

Ecclesiastes 3:18 I also said to myself, *"As for humans, God tests them so that they may see that they are like the animals."*

A Time for Everything

1. There is a time for everything, and a season for every activity under the heavens.
2. A time to be born, and a time to die, a time to plant, and a time to uproot.
3. A time to kill and a time to heal, a time to tear down and a time to build.
4. A time to mourn and a time to dance.
5. A time to scatter stones and a time to gather them; a time to embrace and a time to refrain from embracing.

6. A time to search and a time to give up, a time to keep and a time to throw away.
7. A time to tear and a time to mend, a time to be silent and a time to speak.
8. A time to love and a time to hate, a time for war and a time for peace.

(play "Turn, Turn, Turn," by the Byrds)

Bible Scholars explanation:

"But the unknown should not cast a shadow over our joy, faith, or work, because we know that someone greater is in control."

We Put our Trust in God

James 1: 7 *"Blessed is the man who remains steadfast under trail, for when he has stood the test, he will receive the crown of life, which God has promised to those that love him."*

Times of trouble come to test us.

God is love and so has blessed us.

In peace and patience, we abide

with kindness still for all around us.

With faithfulness and self-control

and gentle goodness from above,

there is no crisis can defeat us

in the Spirit of God's Love.

In the Spirit of God's Love

"There is light in this world, a healing spirit, more powerful than any darkness we may encounter. We sometimes lose sight of this force when there is suffering, or too much pain. But suddenly, the spirit will emerge through the lives of ordinary people who hear a call and answer in the extraordinary ways." Mother Theresa.

"Until you make the unconscious conscious, it will direct your life and you will call it fate." Carl Jung

John 16:7-8 *"And Jesus said to the disciples, unless I go away, the Holy Spirit will not come to you, but if I go, I will send Him to you, and when he comes, he will prove the world to be in the wrong regarding sin, and righteousness, and judgement."*

play *"Thank God I Do,"* by Lauren Daigle

CHAPTER 4

From the Advent to Resurrection: Sacrificial Love to Easter Freedom

The story of the coming of Christ in our times announces the beginning of Christmas Season! Our Best Season. Not just presents, but the presence of God. Jesus' arrival. Our arrival. New life! The good news foretold! The ADVENT Season is all about reflecting on how we can prepare our hearts and homes for the celebration of Christ's birth in the world as it is today. It is a time for faith communities and families to commune together through prayer, reflections, music and good deeds. We are reminded of the true meaning and significance of Jesus' birth. The Advent season invites us to step away from what can be a frenzied time of parties, shopping and commercial noise to consider how we may commemorate the birth of Jesus, one of the Holiest times in Christian faith. It is also time to reflect upon the triumphant return of Jesus at our Lord and Savior's Second Coming.

(play *"Then Christ Came"* by, Phil Wickham).

Prophecies about Jesus are found in 456 examples in the Old Testament (Alfred Edersheim), including the Greatest Commandment in Leviticus 19:18, and Deuteronomy 6:45. The Great Commission was found as early as in Genesis 13:12.

The Advent Season is a celebration of The Servant King. "Behold my servant whom I uphold, my elect one in whom my soul delights! I have put my spirit upon him. He will bring forth justice for the Gentiles. Isiah 42:1."

Jesus came to us as a servant to bring about our salvation and New Life with the sacrifice of his own, and in doing so he set the supreme example. But in coming to us as a Servant and a king, he did not diminish his power; "By no means! "As the apostle Paul would say. Jesus showed us that true leadership requires humility, compassion and a Servant Heart. Our Lord and Savior gave us the template for sacrificial Love. But we do not need to physically die to serve others, we need only let go of a bit of our egos and demonstrate that we value others above ourselves. Jesus shows us that we are called to be lovingly enslaved to God and lovingly enslaved to each other. www.joymargetts.com

During the 4 Sunday Advent season, a candle is lit on each Sunday to stretch out the anticipation of Baby Jesus. There is a theme for each candle: Hope then Peace then Joy and then (very appropriately) Love on Christmas Eve. And Love is not just a feeling. We can fall in love with God and so each other, but love is what Jesus put into action on the cross and it is from the Love of Jesus that we commit sacrificial acts of love. Even little acts of service are big, if done in the spirit of The Servant King.

Isiah 7:14 "Therefore the Lord himself will give you a sign. Behold, a virgin will be with the child and bear a son, and she will call his name Emmanuel." God, himself became one of us. The celebration of Advent is not a Biblical mandate, but rather a helpful reminder of who we are and who whose we are. As we anticipate the celebration of the Heavenly arrival, we are reminded that the Joy of the Children of God is not determined by our struggles on earth, but by our future destiny in Heaven with Jesus and our dearly departed.

The Easter Season is a celebration of the possibility of RESURRECTION, renewal and eternal life with Jesus. Jesus said to her "I am the resurrection and the Life.

The one who believes in me will never die." John 11:25-26

Advent's brilliant dawn is a mixture of sorrow and joy over Christ's torture and ignoble death on a tree; with the penultimate triumph over death and despair in the resurrection of Jesus and the promise of new life for the children of God. The Easter tradition is linked to the ancient Jewish celebration of the Passover in which a plague of death to Israel's oldest sons passed over their homes by the blood of lambs applied to the doorframes. Jesus' death on the cross was and is referred to as "The Blood of the lamb" We are saved by the sacrifice of the blood of Jesus and his blood sacrifice ended the need for sacrificial animals. Jesus' "Last Supper before his crucifixion was a Passover celebration.

And Jesus said there to his disciples in Matthew 26:31- 32 "This very night you will all fall away from me, for it is written. "I will strike the shepherd (Jesus) and the sheep of the flock will be Scattered. 32 But after I have risen, I will go ahead of you into Galilee." (They had no clue.)

Later, in 1 Peter 3 "Praise to the God and Father of our Lord Jesus Christ! In his great mercy he has given us new birth into a Living Hope through the Resurrection of Jesus Christ from the dead, that propels us into an inheritance that can never perish, spoil or fade.

This inheritance is kept in heaven for you, who through the faith are shielded by God's power until the coming of the salvation that is revealed in the last time.

Play "What the World Needs Now is Love" by Dionne Warwick You Tube 3:10

CHAPTER 5

Commandment to Commission-
Order to opportunity

The Greatest Commandment got our attention and launched our journey of obedience to God's word, wisdom, spirit, and love. The Great Commission seemed less of a chore as we mature in our faith, and the obedient moth transforms into the rare butterfly of desire. The calling purpose to spread its wings over the TRANSFORMATION of itself and humanity on earth.

A commission seems to me as much as an opportunity, as an order. Just as a servant, soul seeks to serve in the military and receives his or her commission as an officer. They receive and give orders without hesitation knowing the significant potential risk of severe injury and physical death. Jesus did not need to speculate on the quality of his fate.

The Greatest Commandment flows into the Great Commission and the Transformational Power of God's love begins in the earnest fulfillment of the promise of the Old Testament. Thus two stories become one. God and man, united on earth, and heaven is upon us. Parrhesia Idiotas. I stand for Jesus.

This NEXUS of God and man crowned the most dynamic and consequential human TRANSFORMATION of all on the road to Damascus. From Saul the destroyer to Paul the ultimate Apostle of God's Love.

In his missionary travels, Jesus of Nazareth was both revered and reviled. Even a gracious host in John 1:44-46 *"Nazareth! Can anything good come from there?(In Jesus' time, Roman soldiers garrisoned there made Nazareth a bawdy and raucous little town.)*

Ironically, Jesus was rejected and nearly killed when he visited family, friends and his childhood, Rabbi in Nazareth.

Luke 4:14-30 deserves a full read, but Jesus was in the temple to teach. He was handed a scroll of the Prophet of Isiah, which was about him. He read the verses, rolled up the scroll, gave it back to the attendant and quietly sat down. The eyes of everyone in the synagogue were fastened on him. He concluded by saying to them, *"Today, this scripture is fulfilled in your hearing."* But Jesus was not there to old his tongue. He let them have it.

Rabbi Benjamin and some of the people were furious with Jesus, thinking him just another false Messiah. They drove him out of the town and took him to a cliff where they intended to throw him off, but he walked right through the crowd and went on his way. It was not his time. His mission would not be altered by mere mortals. Even after they killed him.

(play *"Way Maker"* by, Michael W. Smith).

Jesus Christ, as an ambassador sent to us by our Father in heaven, was and is our very own, eternal Way Maker. In Paster Scott Adam's latest book, **"In Jesus Name**," page 10; he summarizes; *"The one who believes in Jesus will perform greater works than he performed for the purpose of the Father."*

Romans 8:*28 "And we know that in all things, God works for the good of those who love him, who have been called accordingly to his purpose."*

Also written on page 17 of "In Jesus' Name", "The disciples are commissioned to pray as members of the family of God in a manner that upholds the reputation of the Father. As new members are added to the family; they assume a new identity and their ethical chores reflect this new identity."

SECTION 4

The Gospels of Matthew, Mark, Luke and John / Epistles, People, Places and Parables. Signs and wonders. Love, hope and peace.

PROLOGUE

Anticipation- The construction of God's word into the Holy Bible: Basic Instruction before leaving earth.

TERMS

Canon- A law or set of ordinances and regulations made by an Ecclesiastical authority for the governance of a Christian Organization or church and its members.

Ecclesiastical – Of or relating to a church, especially as an established institution.

The Mertonian Canon came about the year 200 and is the earliest compilation of the canonical texts resembling the New Testament. In 367, Athanasius, Bishop of Alexandria gave a list of the same twenty-seven books that would formally become the New Testament.

The twenty-seven books were formally canonized during the councils of Carthage, North Africa in 377, and in Hippo Regius (now Annaba, Algeria in modern times) in 393. Pope Innocent 1 ratified (formerly approved) the books in 405.

Christians view the New Testament as the fulfillment of the Promise of the Old Testament. Matthew 1:22-23 "All this took place to fulfill what the Lord said through the prophets. The Virgin Mary will conceive and give birth to a son, and they will call him Immanuel, which means, God be with us." Isiah 7:14

In Isiah 42:1 The prophet describes the missions of Jesus. "Here is my servant, whom I uphold; my chosen one in whom I delight. I will put my spirit on him, and he will bring justice to the nations."

Isiah 42:6 *"I, the Lord have called you in righteousness; I will take hold of your hand. I will keep you and I will make you to be a Covenant for the people and a light for the Gentiles, to open the eyes that are blind, to free captives from prison and to release from the dungeon those who sit in darkness. Blessed is the servant who esteems himself no more highly when he is praised and exalted by people, than when he is considered worthless, foolish or to be despised; since what a man is before God; that he IS, and nothing more."*

(play, *"Mary Did You Know"* by, Pentatonix / official video).

The Mission

Jesus came to earth to preach the Good News, to give people an understanding of the Kingdom of God and the eternal HOPE that we have through him. I thank you God for the Greatest Story ever told, the life and lesson of your Son, Jesus Christ, who died on the cross that we might be forgiven of our sins but only by your grace Father God, has we totally place all our trust and faith in Jesus for our salvation.

As we saw in George Eldon Ladd's book, *"The Gospel of the Kingdom,"* Jesus came to rebuke Satan, not to destroy tyrannical Rome or change the political order of the world. **He came to change the spiritual order of men and women.**

(play *"Name of Jesus"* by Chris Tomlin).

Service in Jesus Name

Philippians 2: 3-8 *"Do nothing out of vain conceit, rather in humility, value others above yourselves, not looking to your own interest, but each of you to the interests of the others. I see your relationships with one another; have the same mindset as Christ Jesus. Who being in the very nature of God, did not consider equality with God something to be used to his own advantage; rather, he made himself nothing by talking on the very nature of a servant, being made in human likeness, he humbled himself by beaming obedient even to death."*

The desire for opportunities to serve begins with a heavenly seed planted in our hearts, or an epiphany from the life and lesson of Jesus Christ, our Savior, teacher, and guiding light.

Service can be simple, small acts of kindness or thoughtfulness (spontaneous or planned). It can be by being gracious or patient when you do not have the time or the inclination to do so. It can be in a place of business with a service worker when we remember that they are not just a means to an end, not just a cog in a machine, but a Child of God (COG) in the human wheel of fortune on earth as in heaven. We call them by the name on a nametag or embroidered on their garment, and their smile is our reward.

(play, *"How Far"* by, Tasha Layton)

CHAPTER 1

Know Jesus in Service in the Gospel of Matthew

The book of Matthew is the first New Testament telling of the life and lesson of our Lord, Savior, teacher, and guiding light. Jesus was of the Kingdom of Heaven, from the city of Nazareth and is at the bosom of our servant hearts. The book of Matthew reminds us of the Greatest Commandment, which is to love God and love others as God loves his children. Then the Great Commission is ratified or confirmed as officers in his disciple army march to the beat of increasing the Kingdom of God in victorious battle with the Prince of Darkness.

Purpose: To prove Jesus is the Messiah – the anointed, commissioned and promised Savior, and the eternal King.

Key verse: Matthew 5:17 *"Do not think that I have come to abolish the law of prophets. I have come to fulfill them."*

The Jewish people were so focused on the prospect of freedom from Roman tyranny, that they enabled the tyrants among them.

Matthew opens his Gospel with genealogy to prove Jesus' lineage to Abraham and King David.

Now, fast forward: Jesus left his family at the age of thirty and prepared for his ministry by first going to his cousin John to be water baptized. John the Baptist was puzzled. Previously, he had chastised some of the Pharisees and Sadducees for their legalist, totalitarian, and hypocritical abuse of the laws for political gain. They ignored God's spirit of service to the average and ordinary people (the Parrhesias Idiotas).

Those who are void of humility and God's grace- Lord it over the people. But still, John agreed to baptize them. Afterwards he warned them in Matthew 3:11 *"I baptize you with water for repentance. But after me comes one who is more powerful than I, whose sandals I am not worth to carry."*

The officials lorded it over their subjects, but Jesus walked with and waded in amongst them us, his beloved children.

Father God, you are Lord, and my master. I need trust and desire to humbly serve.

Humbly serve you, Father and so serve others.

Because you show us, Father, that your true greatness and any genuine goodness in me comes with humility, and it is my pride that comes before the fall.

Each generation of Pharisees and Sadducees are obsessed with the accumulations of power and wealth, but all God wants is for our hearts, and the heart to care for others in the bosom of the Lord.

Matthew 20: 20-28 *"Not so with you. Instead, whoever wants to become great among you must be a servant, and whoever wants to be first; must be your slave. Just as the Son of Man did not come to be served, but to serve and give his life as a ransom for many."*

From Paster Craig Groeschel and Oswald Chambers.

Blessed to Need Less

"Those who are the most blessed are not the ones who have the most, but those who need the least."

Salt and Light

Matthew 5:13-16 *"You are the salt of the earth, but if the salt loses its saltiness, how can it be made salty again? It is no longer good for anything. You are the light of the world. A town built on a hill cannot be hidden. Neither do people light a lamp and put it under a bowl. Instead, they put it on a stand, and it gives light to everyone in the house. In the same way, let your light shine before others, that they may see your good deeds and glorify your Father in heaven."*

The Sermon on the Mount

Please read Matthew 5:12 The Beatitudes.

Purpose: Jesus made an offering to the people of the community; teachings that will build a new world, a new covenant, and a new life. The Beatitudes are a series of supreme blessings. Each Beatitude is a statement about who is blessed and a brief description of what is in store for each category of those who are blessed.

(play, *"Brighter Days"* by, Blessing Offer).

Matthew was a Jewish tax collector for the hated Roman Empire. Tax collectors were notorious for skimming off the top or charging more than required by their Roman Masters, to enrich themselves. They were mostly reviled by their Jewish brethren.

In Matthew 5:43-47 Jesus teaches us to love even the unlovable. *"But I tell you, love your enemies and pray for those who persecute you and if you greet only your own people, what are you doing more than others?"*

Judging Others (the less you know-the easier it is)

Matthew 7:1-2 *"Do not judge, or you too will be judged. For in the same way, you judge others, you will be judged."* Jesus is advising us to be careful not to be hypocrites.

We do not know each other's circumstances. Emotions are often reciprocated. Anger begets anger. Hate begets hate. Love mirrors love. That person who puts out frustration, anger, harsh words and falsehoods could be an otherwise good person, who is overwhelmed in circumstances. Who amongst has not been that person? This is why Jesus teaches patience, mercy, forgiveness, and grace: Unwarranted goodwill for someone, who on the surface does not seem to deserve it.

"Around the Year" with Emmet Fox. Emmet Fox's devotional, for May 20.

How Do You feel?

"Really there are only two feelings: love and fear. Anger is really fear in disguise. In chemistry, we occasionally find the same substance occurring under completely different appearances."

In nature, carbon is a non-metallic element that can also express itself as part of a coal, soot, or petroleum, or as a graphite or diamonds: Allotropes.

A diamond is a gemstone, beautiful and deep in light reflected by the sun. Diamonds are born of carbon bearing fluids, which percolate up through cracks in the crust of the earth. They go through a great TRANSFORMATION under tremendous pressure and heat to become the hardest naturally formed element on God's green earth.

Emmet continues; *"In the same way anger, hatred, jealousy, criticism, egotism are allotropic forms of fear.* Joy, interest, the feeling of success and accomplishment, affection, fondness, tenderness, endearment, attachment, intimacy; are all allotropic forms of love. The difference between the two feelings is that love is always creative, and fear is always destructive.

John 4:16 *"God is love, and he that dwelleth in Love, dwelleth in God, and God in him."*

> (play *"Let Love Win"* by, Andrew Ripp (YouTube -Tim Britton).

In Mattthew 11:2 (as we may recall from the *"Gospel of the Kingdom,"* by George Eldon Ladd), Jesus' cousin, John the Baptist was in a Roman prison. Even he was burdened with doubt and so sent his disciples to find Jesus and ask if he really was the promised Messiah.

When found, Jesus responded in the affirmative and added in Matthew 11:6 *"Blessed is anyone who is not offended by me".* And yet, so many were *offended, angered, and driven to extreme and deadly prejudice.*

Then and in our time; Jesus was grossly misunderstood, misrepresented, threatened and abused. I think many of us can relate

to mental and physical abuse in childhood. In our young minds, it may have even felt like being crucified, embarrassed amongst our peers. We felt unknown and lost. Nonpersons. This is why fellowship relationships are so important to God. God grieved for his son, who is as much in us as we in him. Just as we need God, so we need each other. We grow more effectively in our faith when we grow together. If two heads are better than one, a Bible study group is the power of love and accountability; Exponentially to the power of One God, One Jesus and in the cohesion of the Holy Spirit who lives in us: Individually and collectively – In the Body of Christ.......
AMEN?

The first thing that God blessed Adam with was a partner to do life with. In "Heart of a Servant," the author Ron DiCianni begins with this prolog: **Service to Others** "There is an art to serving others. It is found in trusting God for your own needs, which in turn will free you to look to the service of others."

Matthew 11:28-30 *"Come to me, all you who are weary and burned, and I will give you rest. Take my yoke upon you and learn from me, for I am gentle and humble in heart, and you will find rest for your souls. For my yoke is easy and my burden is light."*

(play *"Don't lose Heart"* by, Steven Curtis Chapman).

The Greatest Commandment

Matthew 28:5 *"The angel said to the woman, do not be afraid, for I know that you are looking for Jesus who was crucified. He is not here; he has risen, just as he said. Then go quickly and tell his disciples that he has risen from the dead and is going ahead of you into Galilee. There you will see him. Now I have told you."*

Matthew 28:16-20 *"Then the remaining disciples went to Galilee to the mountain where Jesus had told them to go. When they saw him, they worshipped him; but some doubted. Then Jesus came to them and said, "All authority in heaven and earth has been given to me. Therefore, go and make disciples of all nations, baptizing them in the name of the Father, and of the Son, and of the Holy Spirit, and teach them to obey everything that I have commanded you. And surely, I am with you always, to the very end of age."*

So is our TRANSFORMATION! We progress in commands of obedience. In our servant hearts, we love to obey, because in our obedience, we encourage, lift up, and empower others on earth, in a clearer vision of the Kingdom of Heaven. It is then, that the Great Commission can be understood, undertaken, and appreciated, as a joyful opportunity to serve.

Citizens with a heart to serve our country and our God given freedoms, seek a commission in the military. They accept commands and give commands of automatic and unquestionable obedience, undeterred by the risk of grievous injury or death.

No greater love is this. And it all starts with what Mother and Jesus told my three brothers and I "God is love, God is love, God is love."

(play *"Perfectly Loved"* by Rachel Lampa and Toby Mack. Written for Women's Prison Ministry)

CHAPTER 2

Know Jesus in Service in the Gospel of Mark

Purpose: To present the purpose, works and teachings of Jesus. Also, to encourage Roman Christians, and prove beyond doubt that Jesus was the Messiah.

Mark was not a disciple, but he was a companion of Paul on his first Missionary Journey.

Key Verse: Matthew 10:45 *"For even the Son of Man did not come to be served, but to serve, and to give his life as ransom for many."*

John The Baptist Prepares the Way

Mark 1:1-4 The beginning of the Good News about Jesus the Messiah, the Son of God, as it is written in Isaiah (the prophet). *"I will send my messenger ahead of you, who will prepare your way. A voice is calling in the wilderness, preaching a baptism of repentance for the forgiving of sins. The whole Jordan countryside and all the people of*

Jerusalem went out to him. Confessing their sins, they were baptized by him in the Jordon River."

Water baptism is an important sacrament of the faith growing heart of my church. Every so often an announcement will be made, and an invitation is offered for the opportunity to be water baptized on the following Sunday. I almost stood up a couple of times, but I wanted to make sure that the time was right for me. I did not want to come back up out of the water just feeling wet.

There was then a change in the Mid-Town Campus of Our Saviors church. Our paster there needed rest, so Pastor Scott transferred from the Broussard Campus to his new flock. After a few weeks, Pastor Scott changed the approach to water baptism. At the beginning of a service, he read scripture that supported water baptism. He gave us encouragement to confirm to the world (and ourselves), that we are committed followers of Jesus. Pastor Scott then announced our appointment of opportunity to receive the Holy Spirit- not next Sunday, but that day. Now! My hand shot up into the air. It was my time. Clothing suitable for dipping was provided. I wondered what the Anabaptist's ritual word to us would be. I never heard of them.

As I approached the baptismal, the crowd noise faded out and once in the water, I could see the baptizers' lips move but there was no sound.

My thumb and index finger barely met at my nose as I was forced beneath the water. I was there and not there. I was dissociative; somewhere in between two distinct personal states. And when I came back up from beneath, I was no longer me. My servant heart took a baby step, but I was bumbling in the wrong direction to exit the tub. The baptizer grasped me by the shoulders and turned me about face.

Out of the tub, someone handed me my bag of dry clothes and a towel. Still no sound. And then I heard a voice, as if from a great distance; it was my friend Lonnie saying "Stan, Stan." The sound had switched back on. The crowd was lively. I was soaked from the inside out.

Acts 2:38 Peter replied, *"Repent and be baptized, every one of you, in the name of Jesus Christ for the forgiveness of your sins, and you will receive the Gift of the Holy Spirit."*

(play *"Born Again"* by Austin French.")

Mark 1:9 *"At the time that Jesus came from Nazareth in Galilee and was baptized by John in the Jordan. Just as Jesus was coming out of the water, he saw heaven being torn open and an angel descending on him like a dove. And a voice came from heaven, you are my Son, whom I love. With you, I am well pleased."*

(play *"The River"* by, Jordan Feliz).

It may not have been necessary for Jesus to get water baptized. He was already a part of the Holy Spirt Trinity with God the Father. He did not need to sacrifice himself to the whip, the nails, and the cross; but he did. This is so that we do not need to literally die to be saved.

Jesus died for us so that we only must die to our sins and our old selves to inherit spiritual rebirth (saved for a new life), coming to know God, finding freedom, discovering our purpose, and making a difference in the servant heart.

It is as Simple as A, B, C

A: Admit to God we are sinners and have fallen short of the glory of God.

B: Believe that Jesus died for our sins, so that we do not die in our sinning.

C: Confess belief in Jesus as our Lord and Savior of our lives by repenting of our sins and placing all trust in Him and in God's grace to receive new life.

If you are ready to follow these steps, you will receive them in a church and then pray this prayer with the congregation of believers. Let us pray this prayer together, individually, and collectively in the Body of Christ, and in the context of our journey together in these chapters.

Please share this prayer with me

"Dear Lord Jesus, you are the Son of God. You took my sin, my shame, and my guilt when you died for me. You rose from the dead to give me a place in Heaven, a purpose on earth and a relationship with God the Father.

Today, Lord Jesus, I turn from sins as a born-again child of God. I confess that God is my Holy Father, Jesus is my Savior, the Holy Spirt is my helper, and Heaven is now my home.

In Jesus name we pray, Amen"

(play *"Running Home"* by, Cochren & Co.)

April 12, Wednesday evening

I went to bed last night with an uneasy spirit, something was missing, and I was uncertain as to what it might be.

April 13, 2023, From Emmet Fox Daily Devotional/**Around the year with Emmet Fox**

Emmet Fox (1886-1951) was one of the most influential spiritual leaders of the twentieth Century. In todays Emmet Fox Devotional, a valuable lesson in the Beatitudes:

Matthew 5:9 *"Blessed are the peacemakers; for they shall be called the children of God."*

As we may recall, a beatitude describes the blessedness of those who have certain qualities or experiences particular to those belonging to the Kingdom of Heaven. Mr. Fox describes the beatitude of the peacemakers as the opportunity to receive an invaluable and practical lesson in the art of prayer. He says "Prayer is our only means of returning to communion with God. Prayer is the only real action in the full sense of the word because prayer is the only thing that changes one's character. When such a change takes place, you become a different person, and therefore, for the rest of your life (we) will act in a different way."

Watch your thoughts, they become your words.

Watch your words, they become your actions.

Watch your actions, they become your habits.

Watch your habits, they become your character.

Watch your character, for it becomes your destiny.

Romans 12:2 *"Do not conform to the patterns of this world but be TRANSFORMED by the renewing of your minds."*

(play *"Jesus Changed My Life"* by, Kate Nicole)

The Transformation

Mark 9:2-3 *"After six days (resurrected) Jesus took Peter, James, and John with him and led them up a high mountain where they were all alone. There Jesus was transfigured before them. His clothes became dazzling white, and there appeared before them Elijah."*

The transfiguration revealed Jesus' divine nature. God's voice exalted him above Moses and Elijah as the long-awaited Messiah with full divine authority.

Breaking Chains – New Life

Question: Who on earth would like a better life, speaking not of earthly things, but of higher things and a higher existence in which anger and fear are rare? A better life in coming to know the spirit of your best self and purpose.

2 Corinthians 5:17 *"Therefore if anyone is in Christ, he is a new creature. Old things have passed away an behold, all things have become new."*

New life exists in the freedom of brotherhood, a fellowship of broken chains. Broken chains which hold us down in the flesh and distract us from the word and spirit of our God.

Proverbs of Solomon, the Son of David

For gaining wisdom and instruction, understanding and words of insight and instruction in prudent behavior.

Romans 13:12 *"The night is nearly over; the light of day is almost there. So let us put aside the deeds of darkness and put on the Armor of Light."*

Some among us have not been blessed to have grown up in a supportive, nurturing whole and unbroken family. If your life seems partial and marked by disappointment, troubles, and rejection, or even times when all is lost; you may have known one person who just seemed to know and love you, even with your flaws, mistakes, attitudes, and behaviors.

A person who had or still has an unconditional love for you. Maybe has even said to you "God is love." If so, was this a person you could be comfortable with and confidentially talk with? Spill your guts to? Was this someone who would be stern and direct with you, without judging you, or putting you down? If this is so,… if this is true,…. then you have known the Love of God.

**The Kingdom of Heaven tells us
"Correction is Not Rejection."**

(This is a powerful message in jail ministry.)

(play *"For the Love of God"* by, Andrew Ripp)

(play "Chain Breaker" by, Zack Williams)

CHAPTER 3

Know Jesus and Service in The Book of Luke

Purpose: To offer an accurate account of the life of Jesus Christ, who was the perfect human and our Savior, our teacher, and our guiding light.

Luke was a Greek Physician, and the only known Gentile (non-Jew) author of any of the books of the New Testament. He was a close companion of the Apostle Paul. He also wrote Acts, the sequel to this Gospel that follows the last of the four Gospels from Jesus' disciple John.

Key Verse: Luke 9:9-10 *"Jesus said to him, today salvation has come to this house, because this man too is a son of Abraham, for the Son of Man came to seek and save the lost."*

(play *"Rescue"* by Lauren Daigle).

Introduction

In addition to being a medical doctor, Luke was a historian and documentarian of Bible history. As a scientist he was incredibly detailed in his study and explication of the Messianic Prophesies of the Old Testament. He meticulously described the appearance of an angel who proclaimed the upcoming birth of baby Jesus and his first cousin John who would become John the Baptist.

Luke wrote extensively about Jesus and how he entered human history and lived the perfect example of a human, and later, the perfect sacrifice, and the perfect leader to deliver us from our sins to be spiritually saved, redeemed, and restored to the new life in God's image.

Jesus Presented in the Temple

Luke 2:22-30 *"When the time came for purification rites as required by the law of Moses, Joseph, and Mary took him to Jerusalem to present him to the Lord. Now there was a man in Jerusalem called Simon, who was righteous and devout. He was waiting for the Consolation of Israel, and the Holy Spirit was on him. It had been revealed to him that he would not die before he had seen the Lord's Messiah (and), moved by the spirit, he went to the temple courts. When Jesus' parents brought him to do what the law required, Simon took Jesus in his arms and praised God saying; "Sovereign Lord, as you have promised, you may dismiss your servant in peace, for my eyes have seen your salvation."*

The Boy Jesus at the Temple

Luke 2:41-42 *"Every year Jesus parents went to Jerusalem for the Festival of the Passover. When Jesus was twelve years old, they went again according to custom."*

Luke 2: 46-48 *"At one point Jesus was separated from his parents. They were traveling in a great crowd on their pilgrimage to the temple and back. After three days, they found him in the temple courts. He was sitting among the teachers, listening to them, and asking questions. Everyone who heard him was amazed at his understanding and his answers. When his parents saw him, they were astonished."*

The book of Luke goes on adding Luke's witness and accounts of the life and lessons of Jesus. He described his miracles, his supernatural wisdom, his healings, his resurrections of the dead, his stories of the fruits of faith, his calming of storms, his casting out of demons, his maturation and ministry of the disciples, and the feeding of the five thousand with five loaves of bread and two fish. Jesus predicting his own death, his transfiguration, his teaching of the Lord's Prayer, and his empowering word.

Do Not Worry

Luke 12:22-25 *"Then Jesus said to his disciples, therefore I tell you, do not worry about your life, what you will eat, or about your body, or about what you will wear. For life is more than food, and the body more than clothes. Consider the ravens, they do not sow or reap, they have no storeroom barn, yet God feeds them. And how much more valuable you are than birds. Who of you by worrying can add a single hour to your life?"*

(play *"His Eye is on the Sparrow,"* by Gladys Knight, YouTube; The Kennedy Center).

Transcendent Joy

Please recite and share this prayer with me - Us
"Father, I pray for us all, the transcendent love, peace, and joy of Jesus Christ.
Not merely a joy that is dependent of life's circumstances,
but the empowering and transcendent joy of Jesus that delights in,
or overcomes each of life circumstances accordingly,
and by your will and purpose for we, your children on earth."

(play *"Overcomer"* by, Mandisa)

CHAPTER 4

Know Jesus in Service in the Gospel of John

Purpose: To prove conclusively that Jesus is the Son of God and that all who believe in him will have eternal life.

Key Verse: Luke 20:30-31 *"Jesus preformed many other signs in the presence of his disciples, which are not recorded in this book. But these are written that you may believe that Jesus is the Messiah, the Son of God, and by believing; you may have life in his name."*

And then he came in the flesh to speak in the universe called planet Earth. The mighty creator became a part of the creation, limited by the time and space and subject to aging, sickness, injury, and death. But propelled by love, he came to rescue and save those of us who were lost (me), and to give them (us), the gift of eternal life. He is the Word, he is Jesus, the Messiah, the Christ.

God Became Human

John 1:1-5 *"In the beginning was the word, and the Word was with God, and the Word was God. He was with God in the beginning. Through him all things are made; without him nothing was made that has been made. In him was Life, and that Life was the light of all mankind. The light shines in the darkness and the darkness has not overcome it.*

14 The word became flesh and has made his dwelling among us. We have seen his glory, the glory of the one and only Son who came from the father, full of grace and truth.

The Greatest Man in History

For a time, no longer the King of Creation but the humble servant of all creation; all creatures great and small. No one is separate or alone. Everyone and everything consequential in the greater scheme of things; before and after the unknown become the known. The word became flesh and in Him was life, and illuminance of hope in the gentle rays of love; unfailing, unconditional, and eternal.

After the baptism of Jesus Christ, the King of Heaven, his cousin, John the Baptizer, gave his testimony of the light to come.

John 1:32 "I saw the spirit come down from heaven as a dove remain on him. And myself did not know him, but the one who sent me to baptize with water told me, the man on whom you see the spirit come down and remain is the one who will baptize with the Holy Spirit. I have seen and testify that this is God's "chosen one."

Then Jesus went about his business choosing his disciples from among ordinary average men. The first were frustrated fishermen.

Against all hope and with no faith, they finally relented to Jesus 'persistent instruction and they let down their nets once more. And they were astounded by nets bursting with unexpected bounty.... And they Believed.... And they became "Fishers of Men."

Many People, Places and Parables. Signs and Wonders. Love, Hope and Peace

Among all the hard-nosed Pharisee's was one Nicodemus who was not too much of a snob to be curious. He was a member of the Jewish Council. He arranged a secret meeting in the night with Jesus.

John 3:2 *"Rabi, we know that you are a teacher (rabbi), who has come from a God for no one could perform the signs you are doing if God were not with him."*

Nicodemus was not yet fully convinced that Jesus was he promised Messiah, and yet he understood and did not gloss over Old Testament clues that he was indeed God come to earth. By the time of Jesus' crucifixion, he had become convicted enough to speak out publicly.

Acts: 5:33 *"Gamaliel, an honored Pharisee and teacher among the Jews; warned against putting Peter and the Apostles to death."*

Acts: 5:33-39 *"He ordered the men to be put outside for a little while. Then he addressed the Sanhedrin, 'Men of Israel, 'Consider carefully what you intend to do with these men.' (Citing a similar circumstance with a leader named Theudas that that came to nothing but his death.) 'Therefore, in the present case, I advise you, leave these men alone! Let them go! For if their purpose or activity is of human origin; it will fail. But if it is from God, you will not be able to stop it. You will only find yourself fighting against God.'"*

And I wonder, if Peter and the others had been killed, how would Jesus' mission on earth have proceeded? The men were spared. Prophesy and God's eternal word and love; the ROCK OF AGES!

Meanwhile back in the darkened room with Jesus, Nicodemus floundered as he tried to respond to Jesus who said unto him in John 3:3." *Nicodemus was confused. 'How can someone be born again when they are old? Surely, they cannot enter a second time into their mother's womb to be born!'"*

Later in John 19:39 *"The earthly body of Jesus Christ laid in a tomb likely provided by Joseph of Arimathea in Juda, who was a wealthy Jewish merchant, and thought to be a righteous man in his time."* Outside the Gospels, he is credited as being the first person to bring Christianity to Great Britain and with building the Island nations' first church.

Rabbi Nicodemus accompanied him, to assist in the preparation for a proper Jewish burial. The funeral service L'llui Nishmat, meaning, "escort" (as in the deceased moving on to heaven.)

Nicodemus found his servant heart for Jesus, after the unknown became known.

Are You Feeling Reverence?

And as we look back now to know Jesus amid his mission on earth, we find in John 1:35-36 *"John the Baptist and two of his disciples crossed paths with Jesus and his dedicated followers, who had typically reacted as on impulse when Jesus looked at them and said, with a confident authority, 'FOLLOW ME! 'They dropped the familiar routines of their lives to follow Jesus. When cousin John saw his genetic and heavenly kin, he exclaimed,' look the Lamb of God!' And his two men turned about and followed Jesus!"*

Have you ever gone out on a date, and stepped away for a moment only to return and watch him or her heading for the exit with another? Magnify that disappointment tenfold for Cousin John! But surely only for a human moment as that reaction was surely assuaged by the magnitude of the TRANSFORMATIONAL power of the love of God, the Father, Jesus the Son, and the Holy Spirit of Truth!

I do not believe Cousin John pouted at the loss of his two devotees. (or at least, not for long) John 3:16-17 *"For God so loved the world that he gave his one and only Son, that whoever believes in him, shall not perish but have eternal life. For God did not send his Son into the world to condemn the world, but to save the world through him."*

> (play *"God So Loved"* by, We the Kingdom/lyric video, global).

Doctor Scott inquires: "Why study the fourth Gospel?"

A: The book of John is an ancient biographical account of the most important man in history, Jesus Christ.

Jesus means Saving One.

Christ means Anointed One or Messiah.

B: It has been estimated that 92% of the material in the book of John is unique and not found in the other three synoptic Gospels. (Synoptic refers to the other 3 Gospels that were recounts of Jesus as seen from the viewpoints of Matthew, Mark and Luke.)

C: John's Gospel shows us the extent of God's love.

D: John's Gospel shows us the necessity of faith.

E: John's Gospel shows us the power of prayer.

F: John's Gospel shows us the blessing of obedience.

Recall in Section 3, Chapter 3 Investigation; The greatest commandment to love as God loves us increases our faith, effectualizes our prayer, adds desire to obedience and leads us to opportunity in the Great Commission:

To lead the lost, the apathetic and distracted to Christ, the Prince of Peace, salvation, renewal, grace, mercy, forgiveness, and transcendent joy on earth as it is in Heaven.

(play *"Burn the Ships"* by, King and Country).

More Epistles, People, Places and Parables, Signs and Wonders, Love and Home

The Disciples Increase

John 1:43 Phillip found Nathanial, who doubted. *"Come and see,"* exclaimed Phillip. As Jesus observed Nathanial approaching him, he said of him, "here truly lies an Israelite in whom there is no deceit." Jesus knows Nathanael. He knows us too.

Jesus at the Wedding Feast

John 2:1-4 On the third day a wedding took place at Cana; an ordinary town in Galilee. Jesus' mother, a friend of the family, was there. Jesus and his disciples were also invited. Later in the evening, Mother Mary advised her son, *"they have no more wine."* Jesus resisted the call for help. *"My hour has not yet come."* But Jesus took the first step into his destiny and instructed the vintner 's servant to draw ordinary water from an ordinary well and filled ordinary vessels.

Later in the evening (John 2:10-11) the master of the banquet called the bridegroom aside, and said, *"everyone brings out the choice wine first and then the cheaper wine after the guest have had too much to drink; but you have saved the best till now!"* Jesus knows wine!

Jesus Knows a Samaritan Woman

The Jews had been long feuding with the Samaritans and were loath to travel through that region. But in John 4:4 *"now he (Jesus) had to go to Samaria.* In passing through, Jesus stopped at a well, Jacob's Well, for refreshment. When the Samaritan woman came to draw water, Jesus said to her, *"will you give me a drink?"* (His disciples had gone to town to buy food). She voiced her suspicions and Jesus answered her, *"if you knew the gift of God and who it is that asks you for a drink, you would have asked him, and he would have given you Living Water."*

John 4:11-25 The woman was still with doubt saying *"the well is deep, where can you get this living water? Are you greater than our father Jacob; who gave us this well?"*

Jesus answered, *"everyone who drinks this water will be thirsty again, but whoever drinks the water I give them will never thirst. Indeed, the water I give them will become in them a spring of water welling up to eternal life."* The woman asked for the water Jesus spoke of. Jesus told her, *"Go call your husband and come back."* *"I have no husband,"* she replied.

Jesus knew that she in fact had had five husbands, *"and the man you now have is not your husband."* Jesus knew her. The woman recognized Jesus as a prophet but still, she was unaware of the being in the presence of the Light of the World, God In the flesh.

"*Woman,*" Jesus replied, "*believe me, a time is coming when you will worship the Father neither on this mountain nor in Jerusalem. You Samaritans worship what you do not know; we worship what we do know, for salvation is from the Jews. Yet a time is coming and has come now when the true worshipers will worship the Father in the spirit and the truth, for they are the kind of worshipers the Father seeks. God is spirit, and his worshipers must worship in the spirit and in the truth.*"

The woman said "*I know the Messiah is coming. When he comes, he will explain everything to us.*" Then Jesus declared, "*I, the one speaking to you, - I am he.*"

From "Around the Year" with Emmet Fox by Emmet Fox

May 10 Inconsistencies Made Clear

"If you were to show an Eskimo pictures of the sections of a horse, but never of the whole horse, he would never know what the animal really looked like."

1) "Perplexed by difficulties and seeming inconsistencies." "a Partial View of things."
2) "Some day (when we have enough spiritual growth). we will come to see that the seemingly disjointed happenings, the apparent accidents, are really part of an orderly pattern." in the horse and the universe, fully seen."
3) And the unknown becomes known, and it dawns on us in our servant hearts.

2 Corinthians 3:15-18 (bible study, Tuesday May 9). "*Even to this day when Moses is read, a veil covers their hearts. But whenever anyone turns to the Lord, the veil is taken away.* Now the Lord is the spirit, and where the Spirit of the Lord *is, there is FREEDOM. And we all who with unveiled faces contemplate the Lord's glory, are being*

TRANSFORMED into his image (Genesis 26) *with ever increasing glory, which comes from the Lord, who is the spirit."*

(play *"Joy in the Morning"* by, Tauren Wells).

The Samaritan woman ran back to her town and gave her testimony, and many believed.

In John 5 Jesus went to the healing pool in Jerusalem called Bethesda where, among the many invalids there, seeking health, was one who had been crippled for thirty-eight years, but the many kept him away. And in John 5:8 Jesus said to him, *"get up, pick up your mat and walk!"* And he did.

In John 6 Jesus feeds the five thousand. Jesus walks on waters but many disciples desert Jesus (in John 6:60 *"this teaching is too hard"*).

In John 7 Jewish leaders were looking to kill him. *"The world cannot hate you but it hates me, because I testify that its works are evil."* Among the crowds there was widespread whispering about him" ... some say he is good; others say he deceives the people. Jesus teaches anyway and Jews were moved. *"How did this man get such learning without being taught?"*

Signs and wonders, challenges and threats all continue to the end, even with hundreds of years of prophecy.

In John 11, even the closest of friends (believers) doubted. Then word came that his friend Lazarus was sick, Jesus sent a simple reply *"This sickness will not end in death."* And in person. *"I am the resurrection, and the life."* But the sisters were angry.... and Jesus wept, ...and then composed himself and resurrected her brother.

In John 13 Jesus predicts even Peter, the rock, would deny him. And when the Roman soldiers took him away; Peter denied him three times. But Jesus is steadfast in his mission. He is still the way and the truth, and the life, and the narrow gate to salvation. He continues to promise the Holy Spirit in John 14 and gives reassuring message of a fruitful relationship with us in the Vine and Branch (John 15).

In John 16, Jesus teaches the continuance of discipleship in the holy spirt of truth- The Advocate- and prayers for all believers.

In John 17, a prayer for unity in a corrupt and divided world, after the torture and crucifixion death of the Christ's body.

In John 19, After the Crucifixion, Jesus appears multiple times to his disciples. He reminds them that the mission is not over and reinstates Peter to his pre-denial status.

In John 21, Jesus asked Peter, *"do you love me more than these Peter?"* *"Yes Lord, you know I love you,"* and Jesus said, *"Feed my lambs."*

In John 16:33 *"In the world you will have tribulation; but be of good cheer, I have overcome the world."* How can we complain?

The typical view of the Christian life is that it means being delivered from all adversity. But it means being delivered IN adversity.

If we are children of God, we will certainly encounter adversities, but Jesus says you should not be surprised when they come.

<u>God does not give us overcoming life, he gives us life AS we overcome.</u> The strain of life is what builds our strength. If there is no strain, we will be less strong. Are you asking God to give you life, liberty, and joy? He cannot unless you are willing to accept the strain. And once you face the strain, you will immediately get strength.

(play *"That's Enough"* by Brandon Heath).

CHAPTER 5

Grace

The mystery of grace is amazing in that we received it even while were still sinners.

Romans 5:8 But God demonstrates his own love for us in this: *"While we were sinners, Christ died for us."*

John 3:16 *"For God so loved the world that he gave his one and only Son, that whoever believes in him shall not perish, but have eternal life."*

5 Characteristics of Grace

1) Grace is undeserved goodwill.
2) Grace is unnatural (natural to God, but rare in the world ruled by the flesh)
3) Grace is unfair (Jesus died by grace that we may receive grace and everlasting life and purpose.
4) Grace cannot be earned by works (but in grace; we obey God's greatest commandment to love as Jesus loves us

and then by invitation; we receive the Great Commission and so embrace God's spirt in the opportunity to serve as ambassadors and laborers in Jesus' legions.

5) Grace is unconditional (no strings attached when we embrace our servant heart, as our energy and compass).

The Alternatives to Grace

1) Revenge
2) A root of bitterness
3) Resentment

Grace is an undeserved favor. Grace cannot be earned, because it is freely given by God in the spirit through Jesus divine work for us on the cross.

The Fruits of Grace

1) Sanctification: to be made holy and set apart from everything sinful and designed for special use and purpose.
2) Justification: God declaring our sins forgiven and us considered righteous. Just as if we had never sinned.
3) Conviction: When receptive to grace; we believe we are directed by God and become consistent in obedience and allegiance to God's heart and plan for his children.
4) Redemption: In our walk with the Father, the Son, and the Holy Spirit; we are redeemed (cleared by payment). In this case, the payment Jesus made for us having given his life on the cross so that we may have salvation, eternal life, and peace.

If we are human, we all need grace, because we are all imperfect and even after being saved by the sacrifice of Jesus, we still fall behind in our pursuit of Godly thoughts, words, attitudes, and actions. We all leak, and we all need to be refilled with the word, wisdom, spirit, and love of the perfect Trinity (the Father, Son and the Holy Spirt).

The only human who ever lived and did not need grace was He who was grace. Jesus Christ of Judah and King of heaven. No one in the time of Acts knew this better than the Apostle Paul, who was as his pre-transformed self, Saul the destroyer.

The book of Acts, which is next up in this volume on TRANSFORMATION, is a historical record set after the history of the birth of Jesus Christ and moving into the birth of his church (the Christian church-our church).

The book of Acts covers the "acts" of the Apostles after Jesus ascended to heaven and was replaced, as promised, by the Holy Spirit who guides us yet today.

Jesus was the embodiment of grace, and he made the Word amazing indeed! Jesus is the Holy Spirit set into action!

No one in the history of the world has been more of an inspiration for the music and lyric of our servant lives than Jesus of the town of Nazareth, where he was a common citizen.

Later in the big picture, of the wider world, he spoke more eloquently and effectually than any human could or ever would.

Jesus shows us, as he showed the common fishermen, and the lofty Saul of Tarsus; the power of love and the glory of grace, to save even the most wretched, including myself, Stanley of Illinois, where I was a nerd.

Jesus calls us by our names and knows us in the spirt of the best possible version of ourselves and purpose under God.

The message in the music gives God praise and gives us pause to consider and pursue our higher power and God's purpose. The Prince of Peace guides us and uses the music of the spirit to empower and hasten us along our path to the Kingdom of Heaven.

> (play *"Heaven in the New World"* by, Steven Curtis Chapman).

If God was the first and greatest psychologist, Jesus was our first and most consequential <u>muse</u>.

Muse:

1) In Greek and Roman mythology each of the nine goddesses over the arts and sciences.
2) A person or personified force who is the source of inspiration for creative artists.

How much do we appreciate the ones among us who have the gift of music, which is such a gift to us spirit thirsty humans? We thirst for beauty, truth, peace, and distraction from the negatives in the world.

Christ is our signpost at the crossroads of life on earth.

Besides Jesus, who is your muse? Who are your favorite musicians, poets, and mentors?

John Newton was such a guide and voice for Jesus. He was the author of the song "Amazing Grace." Considered one of the most hauntingly beautiful Christian hymns in the world. It is estimated that "Amazing Grace" has been performed over ten million times and over eleven thousand albums worldwide.

And like us all, like the disciples, like Paul of Tarsus, Kings and Queens, Princes and paupers, beggars, and billionaires; John Newton has a TRANSFORMATION story. He has a testimony about his yesterday and hope for New Life.

John Newton was a slave ship captain, indifferent to the sufferings of fellow humans just below the decks he trod. He focused more on the horizon and the seas ahead, than on the path that God had in store for him. Amazing Grace would save him. On one fateful voyage his ship was caught up in a terrible storm. Captain Newton faced his own mortality, prayed for deliverance, and was saved. Saved not just from physical death, but by the Grace of God, redeemed and delivered into a new life under God and for Jesus!

(play "Redeemed" by Big Daddy Weave).

Who among us does not need redemption; for the ways in which we think, talk, opine, and act, at some point on the long and winding road.

(play *"Cornerstone"* by, Taby Mack w/ Zach Williams, lyric video).

Captain Newton was transformed into a God fearing, life loving, follower of Jesus Christ of Nazareth. He became an Anglican Minister, hymn writer, and later a formidable and noted abolitionist. He was a newly formed enemy of Satan. He became a voice for God, railing against man's inhumanity towards man.

(play *"Amazing Grace"* by Rosemary Siemens).

CHAPTER 6

Hello Group! A Likeness of Jesus?

It is 06:45am on Saturday, April 29, 2023. I have been up since 06:00am, reading my morning devotional, praying, and finishing my back stretching exercises.

Something wonderful has been happening this week. TRANSFORMATION.

What started out as a dark Monday has gradually shifted to the radiant, uplifting and encouraging light of Jesus Christ. The light started to come up at Thursday night Bible Study Discipleship meeting: Doctor Scott's Discipleship Book + Paul.

It began in communion with ham and cheese sliders, chips, peach cobbler, and the Word. At one point we began to wonder; there must have been an artist in the time of Jesus who would have sketched a reliable likeness of our Savior. Wouldn't it be special to see what Christ looked like? It's too easy today with social media. "Hey new friend, send me a pic!" (Hoping not a photo of a fashion model)

One of the group members scrolled through her phone and found the face of a man believed to be Jesus, and the product of supernatural encounters and visions of a young girl. I did some research as I was writing this to you at about 8:00am, and I found the story on revwords. com (https://revwords.com/encounter-god-akiane-kramarik/).

See the brief "Lost & Found | Prince of Peace" video on the YouTube page of the artist Akiane Kramarik (https://www.youtube.com/watch?v=cHWouIrvwSg&ab_channel=AkianeKramarik). Akiane is a self-taught artist, and you will find her images all to be remarkably beautiful. God was and is significantly in her story and in her artwork. See the Prince of Peace painting by Akiane Kramarik (https://akiane.com/products/jesus).

The Sky Reveals Him

How clearly the sky reveals God's Glory!
How plainly it shows what he has done!
Each day announces it to the following day; each night repeats it
to the next.
No speech or words are used, no sound
 is heard; yet their message goes out to all
the world and is heard to the ends of the earth...
Psalm 19: 1-4 GNT

God is in our story and on the last few pages of this book, I will invite you all to share your story (your testimony) on the last twelve blank pages of this book, as my book becomes our book. We all begin as a blank slate. Let Jesus help us fill in the blanks.

The day after our group; we were blessed to receive a text of the likeness of Jesus, and this attached prayer:

<u>Prayer For Difficult Times</u>

Heavenly Father, thank you for all you have been doing for me Father. You know everything happening in my life right now God. This is all too much for me, and I cannot do this on my own. Please forgive me for worrying so much about my problems and letting my faith fade.

Right now, as I cast all my cares and problems onto you; I give you all my stress. I give you all my burdens. Please take them from me and grant me the inner peace and serenity. Comfort my heart, give me the strength to pull through each day. Help me to not be discouraged, but rather, help me to grow in faith and trust your timing.

Thank you, Father for listening to my prayer. In Jesus name, I have prayed.

Amen.

In John 14 and 16, Jesus reminded his disciples that he would soon be leaving them, and that they would continue in his mission to transform people, which would change the spiritual order of men and women, and so transform the world, people, places, and things.

John 14:12-13 *"Very truly I tell you, whoever believes in me will do the works I have been doing, and they will do even greater things, because I am going to the Father, and I will do whatever you ask in my name."*

As we are becoming TRANSFORMED, becoming a little more like Jesus, and a little less like me, we will become accustomed to doing what is righteous, uplifting, helpful to others and pleasing to God who gives us the command to love and a commission to serve.

And I wonder, how can any of we mortals do any greater wonder, any greater miracle than those Jesus performed on earth? Could anyone among the children of God walk on water, raise the dead, heal the lame, the blind? Can we lift the physically, mentally, emotionally, and spiritually handicapped among us? How will it be when we hopeful and devoted believers come even close to, let alone surpassing Christ Jesus Emmanuel – God with us?

By prayer and petition, by grace and humility, seeking wisdom and mercy; in boldness and by faith, and by belief and dedication and by God and so for each other. **DISCIPLE!**

Lead by example and by expressions of faith, hope. Love and encouragement on earth as in heaven. We move! Mere mortals, we are invested in the promise of the fruits of the spirit.

Galatians 5:22-23 *"Love, joy, peace, patience, goodness, kindness, gentleness, faithfulness, and self-control."* Withdrawals from the bank of heaven.

This discipleship may be the ultimate miracle, the greatest potential of humanity; interrupted by a snake in the Garden of Eden, then resurrected in the hope of the Empowering Example of God's word.

Then Christ came with a humble servant's heart; full of light, grace and hope so we can be bold in the mold of the disciples and prayer warriors that came before us, we march on, energized and fearless, for and of, The Kingdom of Heaven.

A former angry cynic and dedicated atheist named C.S. Lewis described his TRANSFORMATION in his book, *"Mere Christianity, From Atheist to Disciple."*

The disciples will undergo further TRANSFORMATION in Matthew 10:1, Luke6:13, and Luke 9:18-19.

Jesus deemed the disciples to be ready to be tested for their destiny by sending 72 of them out in sets of two, doing the miracles they had witnessed in him.

Matthew 10:1 *"Jesus called his twelve disciples to him and gave them authority to drive out impure spirit and to heal every disease and sickness."*

Luke 6:13 *"When the morning came, Jesus called his disciples to him and chose the twelve of them whom he designated apostles."* (Apostle, from the Greek Apostolos "person sent").

Luke 9:18-19 Jesus was praying amongst his chosen and asked them *"Who do the crowds think I am?"* Several answers were spoken, but Peter answered, *"God's Messiah."*

Let us continue in the writing of our book and sing the music of our evolving lives and spirit.

> (play *"Less Like Me"* by, Zach Williams). Still not sure? It is all good!

> (play *"Haven't Seen It Yet"* by, Danny Gokey).

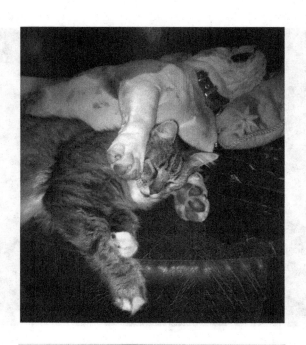

Communication
the Imparting of Information.

① A means of sending or Receiving information from one place, Person or Group to Another. Includes our Emotions, cultural and Experiencial Context, as well As our personal perspectives and perceptions

Communion

The Sharing or
Exchanging of intimate
thoughts and feelings
on A mental or Spiritual
Level OR in An
Intimate fellowship and
Raport with Common
Bonds in Life, ~~mental~~
or ~~Spiritual~~ CIRCUMSTANCES

SECTION 5

The Apostles, the Early Christians, and the Holy Spirit Carry on.

CHAPTER 1

Unity in the book of Acts

There are two hundred and fifty events in the life of Christ, numerically cited in the Life Application study Bible, subtitle "Harmony of the Gospels."

But peace and harmony were a place of refuge and hope for the original disciples (here in referenced as Apostles), and all Christians of the twenty-seven books of the New Testament- The New Covenant between God, and his chosen.

The early Christians were persecuted, many as Christ, to the point of the death of physical life. But hey believed in Christ and the promise of redemption on earth and eternal life in heaven with our Lord.

So, they went out as if there were no yesterdays of brokenness and spiritual darkness.

From "My Utmost for His Highest," a Daily Devotional from Oswald Chambers

"But God is the God of our yesterdays, and he allows the memory of them to turn the past into the ministry of spiritual growth for the future."

So, they went out and set forth believing in what God can do. And they, and we, are all disciples.

Isaiah 52:12 "You shall not go out with haste…for the Lord will go before you, and the God of Israel will be your rear guard."

> (play *"Believe for It"* by CeCe Williams/ official video).

> (play *"Carry on Wayward Son"* by Kansas).

Purpose: To give accurate account of the birth and growth of the Christian church.

Author: Luke (who was a Gentile Physician)

Setting: Acts is the connecting link between the life of Jesus Christ and the life of the Church, then to now. The next step between the four Gospels and the New Testament Letters.

Key verse: Acts 1:8 *"But you will receive power when the Holy Spirit comes on you; and you will be my witnesses in Jerusalem, and in al Judea and Samaria, and to the ends of the earth."*

Doctor Luke's firsthand accounts of the growth of the early church are particularly noteworthy in the boldness of the disciples and other early Christians, consisting of both Jews and Gentiles.

These two vastly different and typically divided cultures became united in their diversity and empowered in the context of the mutual oppression, at the hands of the ruling elites of the times (their Roman occupiers and the Jewish Legalists). Oppression became catalyst for the spread of Christianity.

The book of Acts is about the actions and sacrifices of the early Christians. It describes the establishment and mission of the early church. Luke gives us a brief recap of his Gospel and then moves on to tell the broader story, having personally witnessed some of the most notable events in the history of the Christian tradition.

The Christian tradition is passed on, generation by generation, in the telling of the life and lessons of our Lord, Jesus, Savior, teacher, minister, pastor and our guiding light.

Jesus was divinely certified and memorialized by his works, miracles, healings, mercy, kindness, wisdom, parables, grace, love, and service. He was and is the Truth, the love and in-extinguishable light of the world, the Holy Spirit, and our servant hearts. All these things are of the Fruits of the Spirt, surpassed only by the passion of the Christ in fulfilling his mission from the Father God.

Jesus left heaven to enter a human body; subject to illness and death, to save us from ourselves, even knowing the ultimate sacrifice would be his. But Jesus was never alone throughout his journey on earth, and neither are we. God is triune. God is love.

The Holy Trinity

The Father, The Son, and the Holy Spirit in us. Alive and breathing.

play "*Alive and Breathing*" by Matt Maher)

The Trinity is the unity of the Father, the Son, and the Holy Spirit s three "persons," equally divine.

- God the Father creator and sustainer of all things (all creatures great and small).
- God the Son is the incarnation of God as a human being.
- God the Holy Spirt is the power of God which is active in the world and draws us to God, and to each other.

The unity is foreshadowed in Genesis 1:26-27 *"Then God said, let us make mankind in Our image, in Our likeness, so that they may rule over the fish in the sea and the birds in the sky; over the livestock and all the wild animals, and over all the creatures that move along the ground. So, God created man in his own image."*

Jesus Prays for all Believers (then and now)

John 17:20-24 *"My prayer is not for them alone. I pray also for those who will believe in me through their message (their message – our message), that all of them will be one, Father, just as you are in me, and I am in you. May they also be in us so that the world may believe that you have sent me. I have given them the glory that you gave me, that they may be one as we are one. I in them and you in me, so that they may be brought to complete unity. Then the world will know that you sent me ad have loved them even as you have loved me."* The Greatest Commandment is a song we sing.

(play *"What are we waiting for* "by, King and Country).

"Knowledge of the Holy," A.Z. Tozer. The Holy Trinity (March 4, 2014, Triune Echo)

"Some persons who reject all they cannot explain have denied that God is a Trinity."

Throughout the history of organized human beings, intelligent and curious thinkers have slipped into doubt and rejected anything they were personally unable to explain. Perhaps they were lacking in humility."

When the top of a sailing ship's mast disappeared in the distance, that ship did not fall off the edge of the flat planet.

The Samaritan woman at the well only knew that Jesus was a thirsty Jewish man, until she suddenly KNEW, that she was before the long-promised Messiah! Until Jesus told her, she did not know, nor could she have guessed who it was without dropping dead from shock, that she was face to face with God Almighty.

From A.Z. Tozer: "Subjecting their most high to their cold, level-eyed scrutiny, they concluded that it is impossible that he could be both one and all three. They fail to consider even the simplest phenomenon in nature lies hidden in obscurity.

The Doctrine of the Trinity is truth for the heart. The spirit of man alone can enter through the veil and penetrate the Holy of Holies. Christ did not hesitate to use the plural form when speaking of himself along with the Father and the Spirit."

> (play "The Great Adventure" by, Steven Curtis Chapman, lyrics w/ western background).

CHAPTER 2

Jesus Transforms Saul and inspires acts of service in the book of Acts

After Doctor Luke's recap of his self-titled Gospel; he documents the mission, journey, trials, tribulations, persecutions, success and failures of the Apostles and the growing numbers of devoutly believing Christians. And he witnessed the passion and bravery of the Apostles.

In Acts 2: 4-1 Peter and John are no longer ordinary men but elevated and empowered by the baptism of the Holy Spirit on the Day of Pentecost celebration.

In Acts 4:32-37 The new believers pray and prepare for their new faith life, service and activities under the Father, the Son, and the Holy Spirit. They gave generously to the Apostles, and the needy. But the wicked among them were deceitful regarding what they had and what they gave and, as Peter put it to Ananias in Acts 5:4-5 *"What made you think of doing such a thing? You have not lied just to human beings, but to God. "When Ananias heard this, he fell down and died."*

In Acts 5:12 The healings begin.

In Acts 5:17 The persecutions begin.

In Acts 6:8-15 Stephen was seized when the people were stirred up by the teachers of the law; Saul of Taurus.

In Acts 7 Stephen spoke to the Sanhedrin, giving a detailed account of the history of God's chosen people; their liberation from Egypt, their trails, and tribulations, disobedience and second changes. And Stephen boldly reminded them of the prophecies of the Messiah and how they had rejected, persecuted, and crucified Jesus.

Acts 7:51 *"You stiff necked people! Your hearts and ears are still uncircumcised. You are just like your ancestors. You always resist the Holy Spirit. Was there ever a prophet your ancestors did not persecute? They even killed those who predicted the coming of the Righteous One. And now you have betrayed and murdered him. You have received the law that was given through angels but have not obeyed it!"* (The ultimate hypocrisy)?

In Acts 7:59 While they were stoning him, Stephen prayed *"Lord Jesus receive my spirit."* Then he fell on his knees and cried out. *"Lord, do not hold this sin against them."*

Saul had approved of their killing him. These leaders, so full of pride and murder, knew nothing of mercy or grace, even as Stephen forgave them. Just as Jesus had forgiven their leaders of his tortuous execution. Saul of Tarsus did not know he was to be struck down on the Road to Damascus and then lifted in the new vision; chosen to be the Greatest Apostle of them all.

From abominable hate and ignorance to the greatest proponent of love, and service, to God and so to all of God's creations, both great and small.

(play *"Good Morning Mercy"* by, Jason Crabb/ official lyric video).

SECTION 6

The Pauline Epistles (13 letters). From Epiphany to Purpose

CHAPTER 1

Know purpose, peace and hope in acts of service in Romans.

After the newly anointed Apostles Transformation, Paul's mission changed from one motivation to the opposite. He suddenly knew what Saul did not. Like the woman at Jacob's Well, the lamp was suddenly taken out from under the bed. The Shining City of the hill was no longer hidden (Matthew 5:14-16.)

Peripeteia and Anagnorisis

In the ancient Greek theater, Peripeteia is a sudden reversal from one situation to the opposite. Anagnorisis is a sudden realization (an epiphany), from ignorance to knowledge. From darkness to light. From Saul to Paul. From me to _____).

This Greek theater drama began three hundred and thirty years before Christ and continues today; in the theaters and consistently in real life. It is in Jesus that we are restored to peace and confidence. Many of us have had our personal sudden realization of the Kingdom and experienced other epiphanies. We never know when the next will come, until it does.

Hosea 4:6 *"My people die from lack of knowledge. Because you have rejected knowledge, I also reject you as my priests; because you have ignored the law of your God."*

Law #1 Love God, Love People

Paul's epiphany changed his attitude and his mission from one state to the opposite. From narcissistic hatred to Godly love. From merchant of death to God's own missionary. Paul was divinely appointed to join the Makers Dozen and proclaim The Gospel of the Kingdom that God is love and God's knowledge saves.

Archimedes shouted *"Eureka!"* Snoop Dog rapped "Oh Snap!"

(play *"The Goodness"* by, Toby Mac w/ Blessing Offer).

Purpose: To introduce Paul to the Romans and present the heart of his message before his arrival in Rome.

Key Verse: *"Therefore, since we have been justified through faith, we have peace with God through or Lord Jesus Christ."* (Acts 5:1).

Paul brings the Good News, the Gospel of truth about salvation and grace. That we are saved from sin by the sacrificial service of Jesus and by Grace, the underserved favor of God when we pledge our faith in Jesus and accept the Great Commission to serve others out of love and not for personal ambition.

The Apostle Paul was an articulate, intelligent speaker, teacher and advocate for Jesus Christ and Christianity. Advocate is another word for lawyer, and Paul presented his arguments in person, as well as by epistle, prayer, and petition. He clearly, honestly, forcefully, boldly and with significant effect made his case to all who would hear his word and feel his heart. He helped to save sinners, mold Christians, and increase the Kingdom of Heaven. His commitment to Christ was "for better, for worse, for richer, for poorer, in sickness and in health, to love and cherish, till parted by death."

> (play *"Swingin'"* by, Thad Cockrel, official live session).

In Romans 1:1-6 Paul wastes no time in declaring himself *"an apostle and so set apart for the Gospel of God."* Paul reminds us of the good news of the Gospel promised by the prophets in the Holy Scripture regarding Jesus earthly life as a descendant of King David; *"and who through the spirit of holiness was appointed the Son of God in power by his resurrections from the dead: Jesus Christ our Lord. Through him we receive grace and apostleship to call all the Gentiles to the obedience that comes from faith for his name's sake."*

In the first 27 epistles chosen to be books of the New Testament by the Bishop of Alexandria in the year 367, canonized during the Councils of Carthage, North Africa in 377 and finally ratified by Pope Innocent in 405; the Apostle Paul blessed us with his message of power of grace and apostleship in unity with "all the Gentiles" in fellowship with Jesus.

Romans 1:7 *"To all in Rome who are loved by God and called to be his holy people: Grace and peace to you form God our Father and from the Lord Jesus Christ."*

The word UNITY is mentioned around ten times in the Bible.

Psalms 133:1 King David *"How good and pleasant it is when God's people line in unity!"*

UNITY is a theme worthy of consideration form every moment we spend in the Bible and in fellowship with each other; in church, bible study, small groups, pastor's learning intensives and organized church family activities.

Lord Jesus made this abundantly clear in John 17:20-24 when "Jesus Prays for All Believers" and dedicated us as intergyral with the Holy Trinity. How much more blessed could we possibly be?

> (play "When the Saints go Marching In". (lyric video/live at the Billy Grahm Library.)

Relationship is the Rock and the Hope of Humanity

In fellowship with Jesus, we come to know God and find freedom so we can discover our purpose and make a difference. Parrhesia Idiotas!

Romans 3 - God's Faithfulness

Romans 3:21-24 Paul reminds us that we *"all have sinned and fall short of the Glory of God. "And all are justified freely by his grace through the redemption that came by Christ Jesus."*

Romans 5- Peace, Hope Perseverance

Romans 5:1 *"Therefore, since we have been justified through faith, we have peace with God through our Lord Jesus Christ."*

Romans 5:3 *"Not only so, but we also glory in our sufferings, because we know that*

Suffering produces Perseverance.

Perseverance produces Character.

And Character produces Hope

Romans 5: 5 *"And hope does not put us to shame, because God's love has been poured out into our hearts through the Holy Spirt who has been given to us."*

(play *"I Can Only Imagine"* by, Mercy Me).

Romans 6- Dead to Sin, Alive in Christ

Romans 6:1-4 *"What shall we say then? Shall we go on sinning so that grace may be increased? By no means! We are those who have died to sin, how can we live in it any longer? Or don't you know that all of us who were baptized into Christ Jesus were baptized into his death? We were therefore buried with him through baptism into death in order that, just as Christ was raised from the dead, through the glory of the Father, we too may live a new life."*

Life Through the Spirit

Romans 8:1 *"Therefore, there is now no condemnation for those who are in Christ Jesus."*

In John 17:21-22 Jesus prayed for all believers in him and petitioned God the Father- his Father-our Father…that *"they may be one as we are one. Brought together in complete unity."*

Romans 8:6 *"The mind governed by the flesh is death, but the mind governed by the spirit is life and peace."*

Living Sacrifice

Romans 12:2 *"Do not conform to the pattern of this world but be TRANSFORMED by the renewing of your mind. Then you will be able to test and approve what God's will is - his good, pleasing, and perfect will."*

When we finally understand the goodness of God, we do it.

(play *"The Lord's Prayer"* by, Matt Mahr/ It's Yours, official music).

Love in Action

Romans 12:9-14 *"Love must be sincere. Hate what is evil; claim what is good. Be joyful in hope, patient in affection, faithful in prayer. Share with the Lord's people who are in need. Practice hospitality. Do not be overcome by evil but overcome evil with good."*

(play *"Give me Your Eyes"* by Brandon Heath/ official music video)

Romans 15:1-2 *"We who are strong ought to bear with the failings of the weak and not to please ourselves." Each of us should please our neighbors for their good to build them up."* (NIV). (MSG) "Strength is for service, not status."

(play *"That's Enough"* Brandon Heath)

Scripture for Redemption

First Peter 1:13-14 *"Therefore with minds that are alert and fully sober, set your hope on the grace to be brought to you when Jesus Christ is*

revealed at his coming. As obedient children do not conform to the evil
desires you had when you live in ignorance."

James 1 Trails and Tribulations

James 1:1-2 "Consider pure joy, my brothers, and sisters, whenever you
face trails of many kinds, because you know that the testing of your faith
produces perseverance. Let perseverance finish its work so that you may
be mature and complete not lacking anything."

(play *"You Say"* by Lauren Daigle)

The Bible and its lifegiving scripture can be divided into four movements:

1) Creation- God made us in his image.
2) The Fall- The original sin of temptation in the Garden of Eden
3) Redemption-Restoration through God's gift of forgiveness of our sins and
   Justification (forgiven justice as if we had never sinned)
4) New Creation- New Life

This is the circular pattern of humans on earth, and this is why we need routine emersions in prayer, bible study, regular church attendance and fellowship in relationships with the Father, the Son, the Holy Spirit, and each other.

We lift each other up and guard each other's accountability to our higher power.

Emmet Fox from Around the Year, June 11
"Within you is an inexhaustible source of power if you can contact
it. It can give you peace of mind and above all, it can give you direct
knowledge of God."

This is the message of the whole Bible. It was summed up when Jesus spoke to us in Luke 17:21 "the Kingdom of Heaven is within you."

Matthew 7:8 "Seek and ye shall find."

(play *Good God Almighty* by Crowder)

CHAPTER 2

Unity, wisdom, healing and love in the Body of Christ in Corinthians I

Purpose: To identify problems in church in Corinth, to offer solutions, and to teach the believers how to live for Christ in a corrupt society.

Key Verse: Corinthians 1:10 *"I appeal to you brothers and sisters, in the name of our Lord Jesus Christ, that all of you agree with one another in what you say and that there be no divisions among you, but that you be perfectly united in mind and thought."*

The Christians in Corinth were struggling with their environment. Surrounded by corruption and sin; they felt the pressure to join in and so drifted from God. They knew as followers of Jesus, they had been given New Life, but old ways are hard to give up. Just as the former Hebrew slaves of Egypt were addicted to false idols and bad behaviors.

Moses was frustrated and ready to forsake them and start over, but he took a breath and remembered that God will never quit on his beloved children.

Play *"One Thing Remains, Your Love Never Fails"* by Jesus Culture / with lyrics, upbeat.)

1 Corinthians 2 To the Church of God in Corinth, to those sanctified in Jesus Christ and called to be holy people, together with all those everywhere who call on the name of our Lord, Jesus Christ, their Lord, and ours. 3 Grace and Peace to you from God our Father and the Lord Jesus Christ.

Christ Crucified is God's Power and Wisdom

1 Corinthians 1:18 *"For the message of the cross is foolishness to those who are perishing, but to us, who are being saved it is the power of God."*

1 Corinthians 1:19 *"For it is written, 'I will destroy the wisdom of the wise.'"*

Romans 12:16 NLT *"Be not wise in your own conceits."*

Romans 12:16 NIV *"Live in harmony with one another...do not be conceited."*

Romans 12:17 *"Do not repay evil for evil."*

1 Corinthians 1:20 *"Where is the wise person? Where is the teacher of the law? Where is the philosopher of his age? Has not God made foolish the wisdom of the world?"*

1 Corinthians 1:25 *"For the foolishness of God is wiser than the human wisdom, and the weakness of God is stronger than the human strength."*

Unity and Diversity in the Body

1 Corinthians 12:12-13 *"Just as a body, though one has many parts, but all its many parts form one body; so, it is with Christ. For we were all baptized by one Spirit so said to form one Body- whether Jews or Gentiles, slave or free- and we were all given the one spirit to drink."*

The Bible contains 179 verses about unity. Jesus equates the unity of the Holy Trinity with us as integral and essential components in the Body of Christ and the Kingdom of Heaven. Our faith and servant hearts look for opportunities to encourage and empower those who are not yet saved among us.

God did not put the human body and all its parts and elements together to not be perfectly functioning and sentient creatures with the capacity to simultaneously know and love one another. God is love. Love is hope.

The human body is a miraculous confluence of mechanical, electrical, chemical, and spiritual engineering. Each element effects the other. There is healing power in the body and mind, that our God conceived in a flash of light. External toxins are the enemies of health, whether they be viral bacterial, fungal, psychological, or spiritual.

Healing was occurring before modern medicines were invented. Modern food preservatives and some drugs have side effects. Ancient remedies are being re-examined. Books are written on their potentials in a balance with modern medicines.

(play *"The Healing"* by, Blanca and Dante Bowe/ official music video).

Love is the strongest spiritual energy among faith and hope. Too often in this busy modern world, we might find it hard to empathize with those who are struggling, especially if we think they deserve it. As if we are as Jesus said to the mob in John 8:7 "without sin."

1 Corinthians 12:27-28 *"Now you are the body of Christ, and each one of you is part of it. And God has placed in the church first of all apostles, second, prophets, third teachers, then miracles, then gifts of healing of helping, of guidance, and different kinds of tongues."*

Paul goes on to ask if each member/ part, has all the same functions as the others. He might have said, as he often did "certainly not!"

1 Corinthians 12:31 *"Now eagerly desire the greatest gifts."*

1 Corinthians 13:13 *"And now these three remain; faith, hope, and love. But the greatest of these is love."*

Love is Indispensable

1 Corinthians 13:4-8 *"Love is patient, love is kind. It does not envy, it does not boast, it is not proud. It does not dishonor others. It is not self-seeking, it is not easily angered, it keeps no record of wrongs. Love does not delight in evil but rejoices with the truth. It always protects, always trusts, always hopes, always perseveres, Love never fails."*

Healthy relationships are based on the love of God and are not self-seeking, or lust driven.

Love is the Primal Instinct of Your Servant Heart

(play *"Oxygen"* by Lincoln Brewster, official lyric video)

Recall in Matthew 22:34-40 God's Greatest Commandment when the pharisee legal expert tested Jesus in the law with fake respect. *"Teacher which is the greatest commandment of the law."* Jesus replied, *"Love the Lord your God with all your heart and with all your soul, and with all your mind."* And the second is like it *"Love your neighbor as yourself."*

Jesus DECIDED to love us enough to die for us on the cross so that we could receive salvation in repentance and new life in the TRANSFORMATION.

Oswald Chambers (September 13) defines repentance as "changing one's mind concerning a particular action, conduct or whole direction in life that has been wrong."

In *"Love is a Decision"* by, Gary Smalley with John Trent, PhD; struggling couples are counseled to try again. *"Are you tired of your feelings of love going up and down like a roller coaster? Contrary to popular belief, love reflects how much we honor another person. For at its core, genuine love is a decision, not a feeling."*

Our primal instinct to love is divine but potentially corruptible by the devils' temptations. Love is stronger than hate if it is heavenly love and in Jesus. Satan is just a pimp from hades. In John 14:6 Jesus answered "I am the way, the truth, and the life. No one comes to the Father except through me."

Sunday service is a firm foundation as the Belt of Truth. The house of God has many rooms. On earth, rooms are places for knowledge, scripture, and fellowship. A place to build up our faith in the full armor of God.

CHAPTER 3

Comfort, strength, and reconciliation in Corinthians II.

Purpose: To affirm Paul's ministry, his authority as an apostle and to refute the false teachers of Corinth.

Key Verse: "We are therefore Christ's Ambassadors, as though God were making his appeal through us. We implore you on Christ behalf: Be reconciled to God." (5:20)

(Reconciled means to be restored to friendship or harmony.)

Setting: Paul had already written 3 letters to the believers of the Church of Corinth. He used strong words to correct and teach, especially those who were defying Paul's authority and questioning his motives. (Life Application Study Bible.)

Among the faithful, there will always be doubters. (Scoffers) Or those who fall back into the false comfort in old ways.

In Psalm 73, King David teaches from personal experience. "But as for me, my feet almost slipped. I envied the arrogant when I saw the prosperity of the wicked. They have no struggles... Always free of care."

King David did more than "Almost slipped." He stumbled into the dirt. (We all have a testimony. We can use our mistakes for good or surrender to the enemy.

I asked my Pastor: Why does it seem that satan is more persistent than the righteous? His response was Psalm 73. I found a modicum of comfort. You can go there too.

Is it up to us to take up the armor of God, as in Ephesians 6: 10 through 20. The full armor of God begins with "the belt of truth." And ends with" the Sword of the Spirit, which is the Word of God.

Revelation 19, Jesus defeats the beast. 'His eyes are like Blazing fire, and on his head are many crowns...and his name is the word of God."

Our primal instinct is to love is divine but potentially corruptible by the devil's temptations. Love is stronger than hate If it is Heavenly love and in Jesus. Satan is just a pimp from Hades. John 14: 6 Jesus answered "I am the way and the truth and the life. No one comes to the Father except through me."

House of God has many rooms. On earth, rooms are places for knowledge, scripture and fellowship. A place to build up our faith in the full armor of God.

The Blueprint:

1. Paul explains his actions
2. Paul defends his ministry.
3. Paul defends the collection.
4. Paul defends his authority

2 Corinthians: To the church of Corinth, together with all his holy people throughout Achia: Grace and peace to you from God our Father and the Lord Jesus Christ.

Compassion and Comfort

2 Corinthians 1:3-4 *"Praise be to the God and Father of our Lord Jesus Christ, the Father of Compassion, and the God of all comfort. Who comforts us in all our troubles, so that we can comfort those in any trouble with the comfort we ourselves receive from God."*

Paul also informs us that comfort produces patience and endurance. He teaches us of a comfort that resides in the Body of Christ. It lives in the sanctuary of the Church, and even exists within the cinder block walls and bars of prison when jail ministry comes to visit with the word of God and the Holy Spirit of faith, hope, love, endurance, encouragement, and affirmations. Any building with four walls, a floor and a ceiling can be a church. When two or more are gathered in a fellowship of prayer, the Holy Spirit surrounds and inhabits each being in holy communion. And even from jail there is nowhere to go but up! Spirits are healed and lives are changed.

In mental health and addictions therapy groups, there is a collective spirit of healing. When new members begin to feel well enough to discern it, we see the miracle of body, mind, and spiritual wellness.

The compassion and comfort of Christ gives us peace and hope in recovery and a new life with a drive to thrive in the goodness of God. It is too good not to believe, and too good not to pay it forward from our newfound servant hearts. And yes, Bob Dylan, I do "gotta serve somebody."

(play *"To Good to Not Believe"* by, Brandon Lake)

God's greatest commandment to love is validated and the great commission of Jesus to disciple is the epiphany of our sudden opportunity to serve others and increase the Kingdom of God.

The Greater Glory in the New Covenant

2 Corinthians 3:7-8 *"Now if the ministry that brought death, which was engraved in letters on stone came with glory so that the Israelites could not look steadily at the face of Moses because of his glory, transition, as it was. Will not the ministry of the spirit be even more glorious?"*

2 Corinthians 3:12-13 *"Therefore, since we have such a hope, we are very bold. We are not like Moses, who would put a veil over his face to prevent the Israelites from seeing the end of what was passing away."*

2 Corinthians 3:16-18 *"But whenever anyone turns to the Lord (Jesus), the veil is taken away. Now the Lord is the Spirit, and where the Spirit of the Lord is, there is freedom. And we all, who with unveiled faces contemplate the Lord's glory, are being transformed into his image with ever-increasing glory, which comes from the Lord, who is the Spirit."*

"Those who were trying to be saved by keeping up the Old Testament law were soon being tied up in rules and ceremonies. But now, through the Holy Spirit, God provides freedom from sin." (Life Application Study Bible)

Present Weakness and Resurrection of Life

2 Corinthians 4:1-2 *"Therefore, since through God's mercy we have this ministry, we do not lose heart. Rather we have renounced secret and shameful ways; we do not use deception, nor do we distort the word of God. On the contrary, by setting forth the truth plainly we commend ourselves to everyone's conscience in the sign of God."*

When we care as much or more about other people than ourselves (like them or not), we begin to get into our cognitive, spiritual, and behavioral natures "under God."

Maturity and unity in the Body of Christ means we not only obey God's commandments, but in comfort and joy we desire to please God as a standard to bear, display and live. And Jesus, who loved us enough to willingly suffer and die for us is recognized as not only the son of God, but as he refers to himself- The Son of Man.

Matthew 20:28 *"Just as the Son of Man did not come to be served, but to serve and to give his life as a ransom for many."*

In John 8, there was confusion over who Jesus really was and who his opponents were.

John 8:27-28 *"They did not understand that he was telling them about his Father God. So, Jesus said 'when you have lifted up the Son of Man, then you will know that I am he, and that I do nothing on my own but speak just what the Father has thought me.'"*

John 8:31 *"To the Jews who had believed him Jesus said, 'If you hold to my teaching, you are really my disciples. Then you will know the truth and the truth will set you free.'"*

The Parable of the Prodigal Son

In Luke 15:11-32 The parable of the Prodigal Son (the lost son, who was spending money and resources freely, reckless, wasteful, and extravagantly); a man's younger son demanded his share of his father's estate early, showing an arrogant sense of entitlement and a yielding to the spirt of immediate gratification. He was in bondage to greed and triggered by the temptations of the pimp of hades. He drifted to a faraway place where he squandered his inheritance in a brief period of time and found himself starving in a time of severe famine.

In desperation, he took a job feeding a man's pigs. He longed to fill his stomach with the pods the pigs were eating, but no one gave him anything. He finally came to his senses and came running home to his father.

"But while he was still a long way off, his father saw him and was filled with compassion for him, he ran to his son threw his arms around him and kissed him. The son said to him, 'father, I have sinned against you, I am no longer worthy to be called your son.'"

And so, the lost son was reconciled, redeemed, renewed, and accepted back into the house of his father, and to the Father in Heaven. We are all lost until we are found.

(play *"Running Home"* by Cochren and Company/ official lyric video).

The Ministry of Reconciliation

2 Corinthians 5:17-20 *"Therefore, if anyone is in Christ, the new creation has come. The old has gone, the new is here. All this is from God, who reconciled us to himself through Christ and gave us the*

ministry of reconciliation. We are therefore Christ's Ambassadors, as though God were making his appeal thorough us."

Matthew 28:19 *"Therefore go out and make disciples of all nations."*

This is Jesus' simple invitation to we ordinary citizens of the Body of Christ, with a new life of comfort that gives hope and strength to endure, thrive in and increase the sovereign and everlasting nation of the Kingdom of Heaven.

play *"Say I Won't"* by Mercy Me/ official lyric video).

CHAPTER 4

No other gospel. Faith or works of the law. Life by the spirit and doing good for all in Galations.

Promise, freedom of Christ, life by the spirit and doing good for all in Galatians.

Purpose: To refute the Judaizers who taught that Gentile believers must obey Jewish law to be saved; and to call Christians to faith and freedom in Christ.

Key verse: "It is for freedom that Christ has set us free. Stand firm, then and do not let yourselves be burdened again by the yoke of slavery." (5:1)

Setting: The most pressing controversy in the early church was the relationship of new believers, particularly Gentiles to the Jewish laws. Judaizers were a divisive faction within the early church who were more obsessed with the rule of law than the greatest of God's commandments (1) to love one another. (2) The Great Commission, which was a calling,, and opportunity to participate in Jesus' mission to increase the Kingdom of Heaven and so hasten our walk with the Prince of Peace who saved us from our sins and set us apart to serve one another in love and acceptance of our differences.

(play *"Revolutionary"* by, Josh Wilson, official lyric version).

Life in this world, then and now, requires perseverance. The voices of intolerance for differing beliefs, and censorship of expression can be embedded in the halls of government and in the hard hearts of appointed leaders of government agencies that have the power to silence, abuse and crush average ordinary citizens and political opponents.

2 Timothy 1:7 *"For the spirit of God gave us does not make us timid, but gives us power, love and self-discipline."* Authenticity of the Gospel, Life Application Study Bible.

Galatians 1:1-2 *"Paul; an apostle sent not from men nor by a man, but by Jesus Christ and God the Father, who raised him from the dead. And all the brothers and sisters with me."*

To the Churches of Galatia:

Galatians 1:3 *"Grace and peace to you from God our Father and the Lord Jesus Christ. Who gave himself for our sins to rescue us from the present evil age according to the will of our God and Father, to whom be the glory for ever and ever amen."*

Paul and Barnabas had just completed their first missionary journey to the east and found diversions in the region of Galatia regarding Jewish law and its application to the Gentile converts. The Judaizers were accusing the Apostle Paul of diluting Christianity with the inclusion of the Gentiles and excusing them from Jewish laws, including circumcision.

No Other Gospel

Galatians: 6-10 *"I am astonished that you so quickly deserting the one who called you to live in grace with Christ and are t urning to a different gospel. Which is really no gospel at all. Some people are throwing you into confusion and trying to pervert the gospel of Christ. Am I now trying to win the approval of human beings, or of God? Or am I trying to please people I would not be a servant of Christ."* Amen Paul!

Paul was clearly not a people pleaser or a self-promoting politician. He comported himself as a sanctified set apart minister to the people and advocate attorney for God in heaven and Jesus among us. He made intelligent, articulate, straight forward and trustworthy arguments for the foundations of the Christian faith, and clear practical guidelines for believers.

Paul was a humble servant of Jesus Christ who put God at the center of his decisions, promoted social equality, and spoke truth to power. He inspired generations of followers, disciples, priest, pastors and the like-minded Sir Thomas More; the British humanist, statesman and chancellor of England who stood up to King Henry VIII, and like Paul, was beheaded for living for God, Jesus, and the Holy Spirit. For telling the Gospel Truth.

Saint Thomas More was portrayed as the ultimate man of conscience and true to his principles and religion, under all circumstances in the 1966 Academy Award winning film, *"A Man for all Seasons."*

In Galations2 Cephas (Peter) by joining the Judaizers, was implicitly supporting their claim that Christ alone was not sufficient for salvation.

Galatians 2:11-12 *"When Cephas came to Antioch I opposed him to his face, because he stood condemned. For before certain men came from James, he used to eat with the Gentiles. But when they arrived, he began to draw back and separate himself from the Gentiles because he was afraid of those who belonged to the circumcision group."*

Although Peter was a leader in the church, he was chained to fear of what James (also a church leader), and the others would think. Not so parrhesia as he was at the beautiful gate at the Temple in Acts.

Galatians 2:14-16 *"When I saw that they were not acting in line with the truth of the gospel, I said to Cephas, in front of them; 'You are a Jew, yet you live like a Gentile and not like a Jew. We who are Jews by birth; know that a person is not justified by the works of the law, but by faith in Jesus Christ."*

Galatians 2:21 "I do not set aside the grace of God, for if righteousness could be gained through the law, Christ died for nothing!"

So, Peter had given in to the fear of political pressure and human nature to" Go along to get along". Fear of disagreement is a chain of self-doubt and in-action. Keeping the peace in appeasement is to perpetuate discord, and dysfunction. **Bringing our grievances to others, to outsiders, instead of the ones we have the problem with, is Gossip.**

Proverbs 26:20 *"Without wood a fire goes out, without gossip a quarrel dies down. As charcoal to embers and as wood to a fire, so is a quarrelsome person for kindling strife."*

Making peace is not accomplished in passivity or aggression, but in the assertive style of communication. To express yourself in terms of concern, clearly, and confidentiality after actively and respectfully listening to what others have to say. **God made us with two ears**

and one mouth for a reason! Peter, who was Jesus' rock; had gone soft! *He would make a triumphant comeback.*

In John 1:40-42 Andrew, Peter's brother announced that he had found the messiah. And he brought him to Jesus. Jesus looked at him and said, *"You are Simon, the son of John. You will be called Cephas."* Cephas translated from the Aramaic to Peter; means rock or stone. Jesus looked at the Apostle to be and knew him. None of us are hidden from God.

In Matthew 16, only Peter asserted himself. (16*)" You are the Messiah, the son of the living God."* And Jesus, being God, responded likewise.

Matthew 16:18 And I tell you that you are Peter, and on this rock, I will build my church, and the gates of Hades will not overcome it." We fall back into uncertainty and old ways, even Cephas. Satan will always be the pimp of Hades, but with God; we rise above.

Jesus later established hardheaded, tempestuous Peter to be the first Pope of the Church of Rome.

Faith or Works of the Law

In Galatians 3, Paul finds that the Galatians had become fascinated by false teachers' arguments, as though they had been bewitched by new teachers and smooth Propaganda: the spreading of ideas, information, or rumors that sound good on the surface but are tools to promote disinformation to discredit and damage an opposing voice. False teachers are servants only unto themselves.

Galatians 3:7 *"Understand then, that those who have faith are children of Abraham. Scripture foresaw that God would justify the Gentiles by faith."*

False teachers exploit uncertainty. Salvation by faith or works?... Both!

Galatians 3:10 *"For all who rely on the works of the law are under a curse, as it is written. Cursed is everyone who does not obey the book of the law. The righteous will live by faith."*

The Pharisees obsessed on the law and had contempt for the average folks. They sacrificed their humanity for personal power and prestige.

The Law and the Promise

Galatians 3:16-17 "The promises were spoken to Abraham and to his seed (offspring)." Scripture does not say "and to seeds," meaning many people, *but 'and to your seed;'* meaning one person who is Christ. What I mean is this: The law, introduced 430 years later, does not set aside the covenant previously established by God, and thus do away with the promise."

Galatians 3:18 *"For if the inheritance depends on the law, then it no longer depends on the promise; but God in his grace gave it to Abraham through a promise."*

Whew! Ya'll got that? According to the Life Application Study Bible, it means that the Law has two functions. One the plus side; it reveals the nature and will of God and shows people how to treat others as he desires. Love God- Love People.

On the negative side, God and our Holy Spirit point out our sins and show us that while obedience to God's commandments of the Old Testament are required, faith in the Father, the Son, and the Holy Spirit are the blessed part of following Jesus and our servant hearts.

The more we come to know and embrace God's law and standards, the more we recognize our sinful nature and better contain our sin triggers. And with growing consistency, we can check ourselves before we wreck ourselves, and be the best possible version of us under God.

So, help us Father to not be unkind, or unwise as the day's frustrations, disappointments, setbacks, hardships, and vexing people lead us down a path towards frustration, aggravation, anger, offended-ness, and unforgiveness. Let no unkind thought or word linger in our minds or part our lips as we hear our Holy Spirt- our helper, whisper to us "Be still, for I am with you," or SILENCE! If that is what we need to hear. And you stop us in our tracks, Father God, you lead us back, you call us back by your grace – to the peace of Christ. Father God, we MUST not allow the deceiver to steal the joy we found in you, amen.

In Galatians 3:19-20 The promise of God came to Abraham directly from God and not through prophets or angels. In this passage, Paul shows us the superiority of salvation and growth by faith over being saved by keeping the Jewish laws. (Life Application Study Bible)

Galatians 3:19 *"Why then was the law given at all?"*

Galatians 3:21 *"Is the law, therefore, opposed to the promises of God?"* Absolutely not! For if a law could impact life, then righteousness would certainly have come by the law."

Galatians 3:22 *"But scripture has locked up everything under control of sin, so that what was promised, being given through faith in Jesus Christ, might be given to those who believe."*

Galatians 3:24 *"So the law was our guardian until Christ came so that we might be justified by faith."*

The rule of law is essential for civil society, but not the most important to the God of the New Testament, wherefore God said Law #1 is love.

Children of God

Galatians 3:26-27 *"So in Christ Jesus, you are all children of God through faith. For all of you who were baptized into Christ have clothed yourselves with Christ. There is neither Jew nor Gentile, neither slave nor free, nor is there male and female for you are All ONE in Jesus."*

Proverbs 17:17 *"A friend loves a friend at all times and a brother is born for a time of adversity."*

Romans 12:10 *"Be devoted to one another in love. Honor one another above yourselves."*

There are twenty-five verses about brotherhood and twenty on fellowship in the bible.

Brotherhood: An association of men (and women) united for a common purpose as a fraternity.

Fellowship: The companionship of individuals in a congenial agreeable or blessed atmosphere.

1 Corinthians 1:10 *"To live in harmony with each other. Let there be no division of the church."* I do not think the disciples were that congenial when they first began walking together with Jesus. Pastor, Dr. Charles Stanley stated *"Do you want to get stronger? Get connected. When we face trials, those we are connected to support us and give us comfort. They give us perspective and objectivity and correct us with mercy."* Hmm, where have I heard this before? The strongest associations in human history were forged in the fires of adversity, the crucible of oppression and love for God.

> Play He *Ain't Heavy, He's my Brother"*by, The Hollies, music video, 3 minute twenty-six second version).

Freedom in Christ

Galatians 5:1 *"It is for freedom that Christ has set us free."*

Galatians 5:4-6 *"Stand firm, then and do not let yourselves be burdened again by a yoke of slavery. You who are trying to be justified by the law have been alienated from Christ. For through the spirit we eagerly await by faith, the righteousness for which we hope. For in Christ Jesus neither circumcision, nor uncircumcision has any value."*

Life by the Spirit

Galatians 5:13 *"You my brothers and sisters, were called to be free but do not use your freedom to indulge in the flesh; rather serve one another humbly in love."*

Galatians 5:16-17 *"I say walk by the spirit, and you will not gratify the desires of the flesh. For the flesh desires what is contrary to the spirit, in conflict with one another."*

Galatians 5:22 *"But the fruit of the spirit is love, joy, peace, patience, kindness, goodness, faithfulness, and self-control. Against such things there is no law."*

Doing Good for All

Galatians 6:1 *"Brothers and sisters, if someone is caught in a sin, you who live by the spirit should restore that person gently."* Not passive or aggressive, but in love express concern and bless them with affirmations and encouragement. Let your kind and gentle nature be known by all who would see the Peace in Freedom, Faithfulness, and Self-Control walking in Jesus."

Galatians 6:6-9 *"Nevertheless, the one who receives instruction in the word should share all good things with their instructor. Whoever sews to please the spirit, from the spirit will reap eternal life. Let us not grow weary of doing good."*

(play "The Goodness" by, Toby Mac, Blessing Offer, lyric video).

CHAPTER 5

Chosen for redemption, thanks, prayers for believers, alive in Christ, Jews and Gentiles, unity in the body of Christ, instructions for living, families in the armor of God in Ephesians

---

Purpose: To strengthen the believers in Ephesus in their Christian faith by explaining the nature and purpose of the churches to be.

The Body of Christ

Key Verse: Ephesians 4:4-6 *"There is one body and one spirit, just as you were called to one hope when you were called; one Lord, one faith, one baptism, one God, one Father of all who is over all, and through all, and in all"*

Father God, help me to have patience in my Kingdom of Heaven journey and in finding my proper place in your plan for me. Instead of giving in to anxiety and doubts in small improvements, may I internalize every steppingstone as a blessing set upon the cornerstone of Christ that you have set in my new life. Give me a new attitude and new hope in Jesus Christ my Lord and Savior, my teacher, my guiding light. Amen

(play *"Cornerstone"* by Toby Mac with Zach Williams, lyric video)

Ephesians 1 Paul an Apostle of Jesus Christ by the will of God.

To God's holy people in Ephesus, the faithful in Jesus Christ. *"Grace and peace to you from God our Father and the Lord Jesus Christ."* Paul wrote this letter to the church in Ephesians to give them in-depth teaching about how to nurture and maintain unity in the church; and I think to expose the hypocrisy of prejudice and discrimination.

God makes no allowance in our heads or hearts for the ignorance of prejudices or the injustice of discrimination. Since the Bible is the fully inspired word of God, and without error, our personal judgement formed of ignorance or ill will is not under God and is so sinful.

In Genesis (26), God said *"Let us make man kind in our image and likeness"* means that we should see all humans as equally valuable, beautiful and dignified, regardless of race, ethnicity, color, class or sex."

THIS is the fundamental redemptive quality. God is love. PERIOD!

Question: Do we learn more from people who are the same as us, or different? Studies show that ancient communities with horses developed, grew, and prospered most because they could travel farther and learn more from diverse cultures.

In Ephesians 1 Paul needs to remind us of the praiseworthy blessings of unconditional love, salvation, adoption, and sonship we have been given as heirs to the Kingdom of Heaven and peace on earth.

Thanksgiving and Prayer

Apostle Paul was not only the advocate for love, but the master of encouragement and motivation for us to bring the Prince of Peace – Christ Jesus, into our servant hearts and pay love forward.

Even children of God can fall into conflicts of egos or selfish want. But anger and material things are temporary in this world. Darkness, stress, and anxiety heals with time and yields back to calm logic in the light of Jesus.

Material things turn to dust. But in our relationships under God, by nature, we tend to nurture. It is in remembrance of and reverence for our preordained oneness with the Father, the Son, and the Holy Spirit, that we find the peace of Jesus that comes from the Grace of God and the healing power of forgiveness in unconditional love. Let us turn to John 17 :20-25..(again) *And then pray for peace in the Heart of Service.*

When Paul wrote to the Ephesians, it was to give them thanks for the way they loved one another. Ephesians 1:15-16 *"For this reason, ever since I have heard about your love for all God's people. I have not stopped giving thanks for you, remembering you in my prayers."*

Ephesians 1:18 *"I pray that the eyes for your heart may be enlightened in order that you many know the hope to which he has called you; the riches of his glorious inheritance in his holy people."* God encourages us to put our spiritual stock in each other!

Made Alive in Christ

Ephesians 2:8 *"For it is by Grace you have been saved through faith, the gift of God."*

Ephesians 2:10 *"For we are God's masterpiece, created in Christ Jesus to do good works, which God prepared for us to do in advance."*

In Ephesians 2:14-15 Paul describes a deliberate occupation in the manifestation of unity in one new humanity. *"For he himself is our peace, who has made two groups one and has destroyed the dividing wall of hostility. By setting aside his flesh, the law with its command and regulation."* His purpose was to create in himself one new humanity out of two thus making peace. (Love God, Love People…. Just DO It!!).

In Ephesians 3, Paul describes God's intentional plan to include the Gentiles as heirs to the Kingdom of Heaven and integral in the reception and distribution of god's grace and salvation in the Body of Christ. Paul at least made the effort to unveil his insight into the mystery of Christ.

Ephesians 3:6: "This mystery is that through the gospels the Gentiles are heirs together with Israel, members together of one body and sharers together in the promise in Christ Jesus. Though as factions in a divided world, Jews and Gentiles were chartered members in God's divine fraternity that has only grown in diversity except as political tribes are inconvenienced.

The Kingdom of Heaven shatters the myth of superiority of any one group over any other. The greatest commandment and the Great Commission explicitly and implicitly condemn any discrimination or ostracization of any well living group or individual human being. The motto of the American Revolution against tyranny was E

Pluribus Unum! - Out of many, one. United we stand, and Goliath fell, ...(repeatedly over the history of the world). God knows tyrants. Our times are more complicated, and the world is a clanging cymbal of "me, me, me" in a culture of manufactured and exaggerated differences. Simplicity is golden, Brevity is the soul of wit and **Love is Indispensable** (1 Corinthians 13)

Unity and Diversity in the Body of Christ

Ephesians 4:1-4 *"As a prisoner for the Lord, then, I urge you to live a life worthy of the calling you have received, completely humble and gentle; be patient, bearing one another in love. Make every effort to keep the unity of the spirit through the bond of peace. There is one body and one spirit, just as you were called to the one hope, when you were called. One Lord, one faith, one baptism, one God and Father of ALL, who is over all and through all and in all."*

Then Paul reminds us of the mercy and blessing of the grace God gave us through the death and resurrection of Jesus..." *when he ascended on high, he took many captives and gave gifts to his people."* Ephesians 4:8

How can we not be filled with desire to be an integral part of the Kingdom of Heaven and share something so abundantly good with other deliberate Christians and then intentionally pay it forward to others; thus, saving souls and increasing the kingdom? This is the charge of God, the Love of God and the opportunity of the Great Commission.

In Ephesians 5 we are blessed with a heavenly reminder of the blessings of walking in forgiveness and love with the familiar balance of love and endurance over immorality, impurity, greed, obscenity, foolish talk, and course joking.

Ephesians 5:6 *"Let no one deceive you with empty words."*

Ephesians 5:8 *"For you were once darkness, but now you are light in the Lord."*

We are blessed to receive instructions for human households.

Ephesians 5:21-22 *"Submit to one another out of reverence for Christ. Husbands and wives are encouraged to love and respect one another."*

Ephesians 5:24-25 *"Now as the church submits to Christ, so also, wives should submit to their husbands in everything. Husbands love your wives, just as Christ loved the church and gave himself to her."*

Ephesians 5:30 *"For we are members of his body."*

In Ephesians 6:1-3 *"Children are to obey your parents in the Lord. Honor your father and your mother which is the first commandment with a promise, so that it may go well with you and that you may enjoy long life on the earth."*

Paul must have known that all this Godly commotion would stir up Satan and his disciples of chaos, malice, and deception.

Ephesians 6:1-9 Makes me nostalgic for the nuclear family I grew up in sixty years ago, and the regular extended family gatherings with much more love, food, and fun than drama. Today's culture seems more fixated on, me, me,me; fame, fortune, power, and control.

The book *"Racelift"* by Pastor Myron Guillory describes a transformational journey or restoration of the nuclear African American family in a reflection on the beauty of God's power and grace, expressed by Pastor Myron in simultaneous confident prediction, firm direction, purpose and hope for a better world. It is a work that "aligns with Christs character," and promotes prayer that agrees with the Fathers purpose, values, and visions for us. Pastor Myron confidently predicts these "benefits will overflow to all people." **Racelift is about a walk with God that reminds us that true liberty is in Christ, not Government.** Pastor Myron reminds me of the power and Beauty in Diversity; reflected most powerfully and purposefully in Jesus' walk among us, physically in the first century and spiritually thereafter.

The Armor of God

Ephesians 6:10 *"Finally, be strong in the Lord and in his might power. Put on a full armor of God, so that you can stand against the devil's schemes. For the struggle is not against flesh and blood, but against the rulers, against the authorities, against the power of this dark world and against the spiritual forces of evil in the heavenly realms."* (And Jesus said, "Nothing new under the sun").

Last night as I was slipping into rest mode for my weary mind and body, I tried to think of the overarching theme of the book of Ephesians. Then I heard the rooster crow! So, this morning and in this moment as you read collectively in the Body of Christ, I think we can all agree that in The Pauline Epistles; often written in chains but undeterred by the oppressing walls of Roman prison; Paul repeated the joy, concerns, admonitions and hopes for the citizens of his world and times; and for all the people of all generations to follow. *This is the legacy of the passion of Christ and the Courage of the early Christians.*

Have we realized by now that Paul's epistles to the various churches across present day Eastern Europe and the Western Islamic world repeat themselves? Are we getting bored with the repetitions or are we emboldened to hold a steady course towards the Kingdom of

Heaven, battling the same evils that transcend Paul's era into the next generations of Christian soldiers?

This letter begins with praise for Christ, and for believers who embraced the Greatest Commandment and the Great Commission. Were these the most eloquent and profoundly delivered words of the Bible on discipline, encouragement, and hope? Jesus gave his instructions on how to pray to his disciples in Matthew 6:9-14. *I am glad it was repeated in Luke 11!*

Our Father who art in Heaven, hallowed by thy name
Your Kingdom come, thy will be done
On earth, as it is in heaven
And give us this day, our daily bread
And forgive us our trespasses
As we forgive those, who trespass against us
And lead us not into temptation
But deliver us from evil
For thine is the Kingdom, the Power, and the Glory
Forever, and ever. Amen

(play *"The Lord's Prayer (It's Yours)* "by, Matt Maher, official music video)

God did not create humans to be Kingdom of Heaven robots. God gave us the Greatest commandment and Jesus blessed us with the opportunity of the Great Commission that we might discover the best possible versions of ourselves and then naturally and voluntarily internalize and walk in the mission of creation.

Michele Pasley, Matin Theology and Ministry at Grand Canyon University asks: "Dear Faculty, why did God create the world if we are all going to die?" January 22, 2019.

The Theophilus Letters

Theophilus Ben Ananus was a high priest and may have played a significant role in the ministry of Luke as a wealthy patron and recipient of letters from Luke that became the Epistles in the books of Luke and Acts in the Holy Bible.

Luke wrote to Theophilus with intention to leading Theophilus, a lost man to faith in Christ. In an article by Got Questions Ministries: *"Who was Theophilus at the beginning of Luke and Acts."* The author writes, "the name Theophilus means 'loved by God' This has led some to believe that Theophilus is just a generic title that applies to all Christians. However, from Luke and Acts, it seems clear that Luke is writing to a specific individual... (and), for all Christians for all centuries." (questions.org).

Luke 1:1-4 *"Many have undertaken to draw up an account of things that have been fulfilled among us. With this in mind, since I, myself, have carefully investigated everything from the beginning. I too decided to write an orderly account for you, most excellent Theophilus."*

Acts 1:1 *"In my former book, Theophilus, I wrote about all that Jesus began to do and to teach. Until the day he was taken up to heaven, after giving instructions through the Holy Spirit to the apostles he had chosen."*

In an extra- Biblical epistle Luke wrote to his friend of the absolute benevolence of God, who is so full of all that is good, that it overflows. He created people out of love for the purpose of sharing love. People who were created to love God and each other.

CHAPTER 6

Thanksgiving and Prayer. In Chains for Christ. Life Worthy of the Gospel. Christ's Humility. Paul's Example. Steadfast in Unity and Final Exhortations in the book of Philippians.

Of the Apostle Paul's written works of service to the Kingdom of Heaven, thirteen were among the twenty-seven books formally canonized during the Councils of Carthage, North Africa in 377 and later ratified (formally approved) by Pope Innocent in 405AD.

Of Paul's 13 Epistles; Ephesians, Philippians, Colossians, and Philemon were all written from prison.

Purposes: To thank the Philippians for the gift they had sent him and to strengthen believers by showing them that true joy comes from Jesus Christ alone.

Key Verse: *"Rejoice in the Lord always. I will say again: Rejoice!"* (Philippians 4:4)

Philippians is Paul's Joy Letter. He encourages us to pray thanksgiving to Jesus and so experience gratitude and joy in remembrance of our ultimate liberation from sin, manifest in Jesus' ultimate suffering, sacrifice and death of the cross.

1 Joy in Suffering (Life Application Study Bible)

Philippians 1:1-2 From Paul and his protégé', Timothy, servants of Christ Jesus, *"To all God's holy people in Christ Jesus at Philippi. Grace and peace be with you from God our Father and the Lord Jesus Christ."*

Paul wants to encourage us, lift us up and motivate us to perseverance in our faith in the Kingdom of God and in resistance to the ever-present forces of opposition to the oneness of unity in the Holy Trinity and each other. Paul shows us by word and by example, that faith leads to joy, and that true joy, while not always born out of our circumstances, often comes from the restoration and renewal that God works in our lives through the life lesson and sacrifice of Jesus Christ. Paul reminds us of the imperative of UNITY among believers in a chaos driven world (then and still today). If we walk in love and mercy, we resist the pressures to categorize, judge and cancel each other.

Under God we recognize and appreciate the beauty and blessings of a diverse society. Through the blessings of the Holy Spirit within us, individually and collectively in the body of Christ, we appreciate that, in the midst of our uniqueness, we are united in what matters most. We are all beloved children of God In our shared pursuit of peace in the spirit love in our shared faith and collective success in life, work, and relationships.

(play "Relate" by, For King and Country, official lyrics).

Thanksgiving and Prayer

Philippians 1:3-6 "I thank God every time I remember you. *In all my prayers for all of you, I always pray with joy, because of your partnership with the Gospel form the first day until now. Being confident of this, that he who began a good work in you will carry it on to completion until the day of Christ Jesus.*"

Paul's Chains

Philippians 1:12-14 *"Now I want you to know, brothers and sisters, that what has happened to me has served to advance the gospel. As a result, it has become clear throughout the whole palace guard and to everyone else that I am in chains for Christ. And because of my chains, most of the brothers and sisters have become confident in the Lord and dare more to proclaim the Gospel without fear."*

Paul recognized that some preach Christ out of envy and rivalry, but others out of goodwill. "But what does it matter. The important thing is that Christ is preached." AMEN PAUL! In this we see the unity and maturity in the Body of Christ he preached in Ephesians 4. In Paul's patience with and mercy for the insincere and self-serving Christ talkers, we see that maturity and forbearance alive in Paul for the sake of proclaiming the gospel, increasing the Kingdom, and speaking the love of Jesus. Paul preaches, teaches, and demonstrates by example: A Life worthy of the Gospel while Imitating Christ's Humility in Philippians 1:27-30 and 2:1-11.

Philippians 1:27 *"Whatever happens conduct yourselves in a manner worthy of the good news of Christ. Then, whether I come and see you or only hear about you, I will know that you stand firm in the One Spirit; striving together as one."* E Pluribus Unum!

Philippians 2:1-11 *"Therefore if you have any encouragement from being united with Christ, if any comfort from his love, if any common sharing in the spirit, if any tenderness and compassion, then make my joy complete by being likeminded, having the same love, being in one sprit, and of one mind. Do nothing out of selfish ambition or vain conceit. Rather, in humility value others above yourself."*

In Philippians 3, Paul makes his case for putting our confidence in Christ and doubts in the temptations and distractions of the flesh, in which his and our losses were many. Paul, the other disciples, apostles, and early Christian believers were scorned, persecuted, beaten, jailed, stoned, and executed under the law. Before Paul's monumental TRANSFORMATION, from his alter-ego-Saul; he was on the other side of that dynamic.

Philippians 3:8 *"What is more, I consider everything a loss because of the surpassing worth of knowing Christ Jesus my Lord, for whose sake I have lost all things. I consider them garbage, that I may gain Christ."*

Philippians 4:4-9 *"Rejoice in the Lord always. I will say again: Rejoice! Let your gentleness be evident to all. The Lord is near. Do not be anxious about anything, but in every situation by prayer and petition, with Thanksgiving, present your request to God. And the peace of God, which transcends all understanding, will guard your hearts and your minds in Christ Jesus*

. Finally, brothers and sisters, whatever is right, whatever is pure, whatever is lovely, whatever is admirable, if anything is excellent or praiseworthy, think about such things. Whatever you have learned, received, or heard from me, or seen in me, put it into practice. And the God of Peace will be with you."

(Play "The Goodness of God" by Ce Ce Winans official video)

Transformational Joy

In times of trouble, Father, I pray for all the Blessings of Joy and Peace of Lord Jesus.

Not a joy that is dependent on life's circumstances,

but the EMPOWERING and TRANSFORMATIONAL Joy of Christ Jesus

that is independent of life's circumstances and delights in

or overcomes each life event accordingly and by your will.

(Play Let It Be by The Beatles. Remastered 2015)

Proverbs 3:5-6 *"Trust in the Lord with all of your heart and lean not on your understanding, but in all your ways acknowledge him and he shall direct our paths."*

CHAPTER 7

Thanksgiving and Prayer, Supremacy of the Son of God, Paul's labor for the Church, Alive with Christ. Freedom from Human Rules. Above Immorality and Instruction for Christian Households in Colossians

Purpose: To combat errors in the church and show that believers have everything they need in Christ.

Key Verse: *"For in Christ all the fulness of the deity lives in bodily form. And in Christ you have been brought to fullness. He is the head over ever power and authority."* (2:9-10)

Colossians 1 What Christ has done (Life Application Study Bible)

Paul an apostle of Christ Jesus by the will of God, and Timothy our brother.

Colossians 2 To God's holy people in Colossae, the faithful brothers, and sisters I Christ.

"Grace and peace to you from God our Father"

Thanksgiving and Prayer

Colossians 1:3-4 *"We always thank God, the Father of our Lord Jesus Christ when we pray for you. Because we have heard of your faith in Jesus Christ and of the love you have for all God's people."*

Colossians 1:9-10 "For this reason, we have not stopped praying for you. We continually ask God to fill you with the knowledge of his will through all the wisdom and understanding that the spirit gives. So that you may live a life worthy of the Lord and please him in every way; bearing fruit in every good work, so that you may have great endurance and patience."

Hosea 4:6 *"My people are destroyed for lack of knowledge because you have rejected knowledge."*

Proverbs 15:14 *"This discerning heart seeks knowledge but the mouth of the fool feeds on folly."*

God, my heavenly Father, and Jesus Christ, my Prince of Peace, continue to "teach me knowledge and good judgment, for I trust your commands" (Psalms 119:66).

From **serenityinsuffering.com**- "How Curiosity Restores Joy in the Lord"

"Having a holy curiosity seeks a better understanding of God, his ways and spiritual growth leading to a deeper intimacy with him."

Colossians 1:13-14 *"For he has rescued us from the domination of darkness and brought us into the Kingdom of the Son he loves. In whom we have redemption, the forgiveness of sins."*

The Supremacy of the Son of God

Colossians 1:15-18 *"The son is the image of the invisible god. The first-born over all creation. For in him all things were created. He is before all things and in him all things are held together. And he is the head of the body, the church, he is the beginning and the first born from among the dead, so that in everything he might have supremacy."*

In Ephesians 4 We learned about unity and maturity in the Body of Christ, which is us and we who are under Christ, the Head of the Church.

In Colossians 1:19-20 *"For God was pleased to have all his fullness dwell in him. And through him to reconcile to himself all things whether things on earth or things in heaven by making peace through his blood shed on the cross."*

> (play *"Nothing Else"* by, Cody Carnes w/lyrics-Colossians 1:15-20.- (This song is long, but hauntingly beautiful.)

In our lack of knowledge and absence of curiosity, we are lost, and our lives were full of chaos, failures, and confusion. "Why me?" By the grace of God and unmerited forgiveness we live anew. We are the chosen of second chances. The gift of curiosity has the power to restore joy in the Lord, if we can reprise a curiosity as little children, when it comes to the mystery that has been kept hidden for ages and generations.

Matthew 18:2 He called a little child to him and placed the child among them. And he said: "Truly, I tell you, unless you change and become like little children, you will never enter the Kingdom of Heaven. Therefore, whoever takes the lowly position of this child is the greatest in the Kingdom of heaven. And whoever becomes one such child in my name welcomes me."

Paul's Labor for the Church

Colossians 1:24 *"Now I rejoice in what I am suffering for you, and I fill up in my flesh what is still lacking in regard to Christ's affirmations for the sake of His Body which is the Church."*

Colossians 1:27 *"To them God has chosen to make known among the Gentiles the glorious riches of this mystery, which is Christ in you, the hope of glory."*

Paul's work was to proclaim Jesus to the world, teach his wisdom and bring us to full maturity in the energetic works of Christ. The potential in each and all of us, revealed and actuated in daily prayer, daily devotionals, Bible study, Christian ministry, and Christian fellowship we deliberately seek in the spiritual fullness in Christ.

Colossians 2:6 *"So then, just as you have received Christ Jesus as Lord, continue to live your lives in him, rooted and built up in him, strengthened in the faith as you were taught and overflowing with thankfulness."*

Thankfulness or gratitude has healing power. Studies confirm that an attitude of gratitude is associated with happiness triggered by having a keen sense of appreciation for rewards, kindness received and other positive aspects of life (research.com>education).

Thankfulness includes regular prayers and petitions to God and Jesus as well as focus on affirmations, which are positive statements. My therapy group members choose the five most powerful for them from a list of fifty. Medicine without side effects. THANK YOU, JESUS!

Then Paul goes on to warn us again, and to beware of "deceptive philosophy" and dark forces of this world that, by definition, are not of Christ Jesus.

Freedom from Human Rules

Colossians 2:16 *"Therefore do not let anyone judge you by what you eat or drink, or with regard to a religious festival or celebration or a Sabbath day. Do not let anyone who delights in false humility and worship of angels disqualify you."*

Father God,

Let no unkind thought or word linger in my mind or part my lips but stop me in my tracks as I hear my Holy Spirit whisper to me "be still, I am with you," and you lead me back to the peace of Jesus. Let the deceiver not steal my joy. Amen.

Living as Those Made Alive in Christ

Colossians 3:1 *"Since then, you have been raised with Christ, set your hearts on things above."*

Colossians *3:5 "Put to death, therefore, whatever belongs to your early nature: sexual immorality, impurity, lust, evil desires, and greed, which is idolatry.*

Colossians *3:10 "And you have put your new self, which is renewed in knowledge in the image of its creator."*

Instructions for Christian Households

Colossians 3:23 *"Whatever you do, work at it with all your heart, as working for the Lord as a reward. It is the Lord Christ you are serving."*

Colossians 4:16-18 *"After this letter has been read to you, see that is also read in the church of the Laodiceans and that you in turn read the letter from the Laodicea. Tell Archippus: See to it that you complete the ministry you have received in the land. I, Paul write this greeting in my own hand. Remember my chains. Grace be with you."*

(play *"There was Jesus"* by, Zach Williams with Dolly Parton/ official music video)

AMAZING GRACE
The gift that keeps on giving!
We pay it forward!

CHAPTER 8

Timothy's Encouraging Report. Living to Please God. Believers who have Died. The Day of the Lord and Final instructions in 1 Thessalonians.

Purpose: To strengthen the Thessalonian's Christian's faith and give them assurance of Christ's return.

Setting: The Church in Thessalonica was very young, having only been established three months before this letter was written. Paul's job was to encourage and assist them in the maturation of their faith and to clear up misunderstandings about Christ's Second Coming.

Key Verse: *"For we believe that Jesus died and rose again, and so we believe that God will bring with Jesus those who have fallen asleep in him."*

Paul, Silas, and Timothy had found noble souls to teach there on Paul's second missionary journey but then found themselves needing to flee an angry mob that had been stirred up by *"other Jews who were jealous"* (Acts 17:1-9)

Later Paul found great encouragement in a letter from his protégé Timothy, who had returned to Thessalonica to find their faith, obedience, and righteous behavior to still be strong for Jesus.

1. *Faithfulness to the Lord*

   Paul, Silas and Timothy to the Church of the Thessalonians in God the Father and the Lord Jesus Christ:

   "Grace and Peace be to you."

Thanksgiving for the Thessalonian

1 Thessalonians 1:2-3 *"We always thank God for all of you and continually mention you in our prayers. We remember before our God and Father your work produced by faith, your labor prompted by love, and your endurance inspired by hope in our Lord Jesus Christ."*

Paul's Ministry in Thessalonica

Paul and his fellow travelers, for the gospel, went to chaotic places *"in the face strong opposition"* and found encouragement in the faithful of the churches they had planted. Paul's letters are reminders and reflections on their in-person ministries, encouragement in the progress they had made, and the blessings of faithfulness in the gospel truths of Jesus Christ as Lord of our lives.

Psalms 18:25-26 *"With the merciful; though wilt show they self-merciful, with an upright man; though wilt show they self-upright,* with the pure; thou wilt show thyself pure, and with the forward; thou wilt show thyself forward.

Emmett Fox, October 3 *"God, in his infinite wisdom, has made the laws of the universe and left them to work themselves out."*

1 Thessalonians 2:4-5 *"On the contrary, we spoke as those approved by God to be entrusted with the gospel. We are not trying to please people but God, who tests our hearts. You know we never used, flattery, nor did we put a mask to cover up greed- God is our witness."*

The disciples were not lacking praise from among the people. Their joy in delivering the good news about Christ Jesus gave them no time for fear.

1 Thessalonians 2:7 *"Instead we were like young children among you."* With childlike curiosity and excitement these later day missionaries worked while they were in town.

1 Thessalonians 2:9 *"We worked day and night in order not to be a burden to you.* Paul and others on missionary trips earned money as tent makers to support themselves and sometimes helped others in His missionary calling of witnessing to Christ. How many know that the encouraging and uplifting nature of our ministers, pastors and priests is infections?

Play" Roc*ckin' Pneumonia and the Boogie Woodie Flu"* by, Johnny Rivers).

1 Thessalonians 2:13 *"And we also thank God continuously because, when you received the word of God, from us, you accepted it not as a human word; but as it is, the actual word of God, which is indeed at work in you who believe. For you brothers, and sisters, became imitators of God's churches in Judea, which are in Christ Jesus."*

Living to Please God

1 Thessalonians 4:1 *"As for other matters, brothers and sisters, we instructed you how to live in order to please God, as in fact you are living."*

1 Thessalonians 4:3-5" *It is God's will that you should be sanctified; that you should avoid sexual immorality; that each of you should learn to control your own body in a way that is holy and honorable, not in passionate lust like the pagans who do not know God.*

1 Thessalonians *4:11-12 "And make it your ambition to lead a quiet life, so that your daily life may win the respect of outsiders and so that you will not be dependent on anybody."*

Believers Who have Died on the day of the Lord's Return

1 Thessalonians 4:13-18 *"Brothers and sisters, we do not want you to be uninformed about those who sleep in death, so that you do not grieve like the rest of mankind, who have no hope. For we believe that Jesus died and rose again and so we believe that God will bring with Jesus those who have fallen asleep in Him. According to the Lord's word, we tell you that we who are still alive, who are left until the coming of the Lord, will certainly not precede those who have fallen asleep (died). For the Lord himself will come down from heaven, with a loud command, with the voice of the archangel and with the trumpet call of God and the dead in Christ will rise first. After that, we who are still alive and are left will be caught up together with them in the clouds to meet the Lord in the air. And so be with the Lord forever. Therefore, encourage one another with these words."*

In Thessalonians 5, Paul encourages believers to be patient and prepared for the second coming of Christ. Knowing, (as we will see in his letters to Timothy), that some believers would fall back to their old pagan inclinations.

Thessalonians 5:2 *"For you know very well that the day of the Lord will come like a thief in the night.*

Thessalonians 5:4 *"But you, brothers, and sisters, are not in darkness so that this day would surprise you like a thief. You are the children of the light and children of the day."*

Thessalonians 5:8 *"But since we belong to the day, let us be sober, putting on faith and love as a breastplate and the hope of salvation as a helmet."*

Recall in Ephesians 6 "The Armor of God". we need to be consistent in our faithfulness to the word, wisdom, spirit, and love of the Father, the Son and the Holy Spirt. So, help us Father that the deceiver would not be allowed to steal our joy. Help us to remember, appreciate and participate each day in the ongoing process of yielding to your word, your wisdom, your spirit, and your love.

There are twenty-four bible verses about falling away from God. Recall the disciples who quit the journey with Jesus because the teachings became "too hard."

Encouragement

Thessalonians 5:11 *"Therefore encourage one another and build each other up, just as in fact you are doing."* Encouragement is one of the most profound spiritual things we can do as descendants of the "Makers Dozen." To encourage someone to press on when they feel like giving up.

Paul's Final Instructions

Paul encourages brothers and sisters in Jesus *"acknowledge those who work hard among you, who care for you in the Lord and who admonish you,"* Thessalonians 5:12.

Thessalonians 5:14 *"warn those who are idle and disruptive, encourage the disheartened, help the weak, be patient with everyone."* Paul has the same servant heart for us as Jesus. The same drive and determination to affect our salvation and increase the Kingdom of Heaven.

Thessalonians 5:16-18 *"Rejoice always, pray continuously, give thanks in ALL circumstances; for this is God's will for you in Christ Jesus, Amen."* There are one hundred Bible verses about being joyful in all circumstances.

CHAPTER 9

Thanksgiving and Prayer, Reveal the Man of Lawlessness, Stand Firm in Jesus, Pray Christ's Message is Honored and Warning against Idleness in 2 Thessalonians.

Purpose: To clear up confusion about the second coming of Christ.

Key Verse: 2 Thessalonians 3:15 *"May the Lord direct you hearts into God's love and Christ's perseverance."*

In this follow up letter to 1st Thessalonians, Paul indicates various events that must preceded the second coming of Christ. Once again, clarifications in communication and further words of comfort and encouragement are needed to keep believers on track, safe from fake teachings, wary of deceptions and distractions from satan and steadfast in Jesus in the face of the relentless lies' persecutions and trials.

1 The Bright Hope of Christ's Return (Life Application Study Bible)

2 Thessalonians 1 Paul, Silas, and Timothy *"to the church of Thessalonians in God our Father and the Lord Jesus Christ: Grace and peace to you from God the Father and the Lord Jesus Christ."*

Thanksgiving and Prayer

Paul loves and appreciates the new believers, and every church he and his fellow disciple's plant. Each is like a newborn baby, crying for attention, warmth, comfort and sustenance in the body, mind, and spirit.

1 Peter 2:2 *"Like newborn babies crave pure spiritual milk, so that by it you may grow up in your salvation."*

1 Peter 2:3 *"Now that you have tasted that the Lord is good."*

2 Thessalonians 1:4 *"Therefore, among God's churches we boast about your perseverance and faith in all persecutions and trials you are enduring."*

With this Paul encourages us that there will be redemption and new life in these sufferings of life on earth (Thessalonians 1:7) *"When Lord Jesus is revealed from heaven in a blazing fire with powerful angels."* Paul predicts punishment and destruction for the wicked and Jesus' glorification in his holy people who believe in him and in the testimony of the first generation of disciples to stand for Jesus.

2 Thessalonians1:11-12 *"With this in mind, we constantly pray for you that our God may make you worthy of his calling, and that by his power*

he may bring to fruition your every desire for goodness and your every deed prompted by faith. We pray this so that the name of our Lord Jesus may be glorified in you're and you in him, according to the grace of our God and the Lord Jesus Christ."

These are all references about oneness with God and Jesus between the Old and the New Testaments of the Holy Bible.

In 2 Thessalonians 2 Paul writes to us about *"the coming of our Lord Jesus and the man of lawlessness"* (2:2) who is the anti-Christ (satan). He encourages us "not to become easily unsettled or alarmed by teaching, allegedly from us asserting that the day of the Lord (Jesus' return) has already come. *"Don't let anyone deceive you in any way, for that day will not come until the rebellion occurs and the man of lawlessness is revealed; the man doomed to destruction."* (2:3)

Word had come from Thessalonica that some had misunderstood Paul's teaching about the second coming of Jesus. Some of the faithful were pulled into complacency and rationalized idleness in assumption or belief in the "lawless man," that the day of the Lord was "at hand," or very soon in human terms.

2 Thessalonians 2:15-17 *"So then, brothers and sisters, stand firm and hold fast to the teachings we passed on to you, whether by word of mouth or by letter. May our Lord Jesus Christ himself and God our Father, who loved us and by his grace gave us eternal encouragement and good hope, encourage your hearts, and strengthen you in every good deed and word."*

Request for Prayer

In Thessalonians 3 Paul continues in his role as the Great Encourager and cheer leader of all disciples; always the lead advocate for Jesus; Christ Jesus our Savior and transformer. The Jesus interruption on the road to Paul's Damascus destruction awakens the Holy Spirit in us and lights our way to the narrow gate.

Matthew 1:13-14 *"Enter through the narrow gate. For wide is the gate and broad is the road that leads to destruction, and many enter through it."*

Emmet Fox March 5

"Don't wait about for God to act dramatically because he probably won't. When people expect a dramatic miracle from the outside, they are really hoping to change conditions without changing themselves; to get something for nothing."

2 Thessalonians 3:6 *"Keep away from every believer who is idle and disruptive and does not live according to the teaching you received from us."*

Final Greetings

2 Thessalonians 3:16 *"Now may the Lord of peace himself give you peace at all times and in every way. The Lord be with you all."*

(play *"Fingerprints of God"* by, dan Bremness, official music video)

CHAPTER 10

False teachers, the Lord's Grace to Paul, Instructions for Worship, Qualifications for Deacons, Reasons for Paul's Instructions, Widows Elders and Slaves, Love of Money and Final Instructions to 1 Timothy

---

Purpose: To encourage and teach Timothy, a young leader and first second-generation Christian mentioned in the New Testament. Timothy is a prime example of someone who was raised and influenced by Godly relatives in a tradition of reverence to God and taking responsibility for the care of the poor and the needs of all members of the church.

Key Verse: *"Don't let anyone look down on you because you are young, but set an example for the believers in speech, in conduct, in love, in faith, and in purity."* (1 Timothy 4:12)

The first letter from Paul the teacher to Timothy his beloved student and protégé, begins by affirming their relationship is genuine and highly valued. Affirmations are "positive and encouraging" statements, that when remembered, received, and or spoken regularly, assist in our TRANSFORMATION to the best versions of ourselves and so aligned with our higher spirits and our soul's true purpose under God. (See Romans 8:28).

Paul knew he was near the end of his ministry and his focus was moving into the role of mentor and chief encourager of, not only the new Christian believers, but especially the young leaders who were motivated by a solemn responsibility and a divine opportunity to continue to the ministry ignited by Christ Jesus and taken up by the first generation of disciples who walked with Jesus in the flesh.

(play *"I Can Only Imagine"* by, Mercy Me, video).

First Timothy is a book of instructions for church leaders and continued warnings about false teachers. Paul and his fellow missionaries shared the intense joy of seeing the gospel being received by many people as well as the agonies of seeing it rejected and distorted, by others. (Life Application Study Bible).

1 Instructions on right belief (Life Application Study Bible)

1 Timothy 1 Paul, an apostle of Christ Jesus by the command of God and our Savior, and of Christ Jesus our hope. *"To Timothy my true son of faith. Grace and mercy and peace from God the Father, and Christ Jesus our Lord."*

Timothy charged (instructed) to Oppose False Teachers

False teachers will always be among us. Proverbs 26:23-28 *"Smooth words may hide a wicked heart, just as a pretty glaze covers a clay pot. People may cover their hatred with pleasant words, but they are deceiving you."*

In 1 Timothy 1:3 Paul advised Timothy to *"command certain people not to teach false doctrines any longer or devote themselves to myths and endless genealogies. Such things promote controversial speculations rather than advancing God's work."*

Mister and Mrs. Pretty Glaze were and are today's enchanters with a secret agenda (plans not under God). Servants unto themselves.

1 Timothy 1:5 *"The goal of this command is love, which comes from a pure heart and good conscience and a sincere faith. "Some have departed from those and have turned to meaning less talk."*

"Arguing about trivial details in the Bible can send us off on an interesting but irrelevant tangent and cause us to miss the intent of God's message." Life Application Study Bible.

Irrelevant tangents are the distractions and talking points. They hide the secret agendas of satan and his minions of self-serving deceivers. The talking heads of this modern world in the 24-7 news cycle are like clamoring clouds of thunder and lightning: significantly nothing. They use the power of implication over explication, rarely speaking directly with the checkable specifics; but more exercised in feigned outrage, animated gesticulations, and grimaces as if sucking on an invisible lemon!

1 Timothy 1:9-11 *"We also know that the law is made not for the righteous but for the lawbreakers and rebels, the ungodly and sinful...*

and for whatever else is contrary to the sound doctrine that conforms to the Gospel, concerning the glory of the blessed God, which he entrusted to me."

In Matthew 4:17 Jesus preached *"Repent, for the kingdom of Heaven has come near."*

The Lord's Grace to Paul

1 Timothy 1:12-14 *"I thank Christ Jesus our Lord, who has given me strength, that he considered me trustworthy, appointing me to his service. Even though I was once a blasphemer and a prosecutor and a violent man, I was shown mercy because I acted in ignorance and un-belief. The grace of our Lord was poured on me; abundantly, along with the faith and love that are in Christ Jesus."*

Oswald Chambers Daily Devotional *"My utmost for his highest."*

December 31 *"Yesterday"*

"At the end of the year we turn with eagerness to all God has for the future, and yet anxiety is apt to arise when we remember our yesterdays. But God is the God of our yesterdays, and he allows the memory of them to turn the past into a ministry of spiritual growth for our future. Leave the broken, irreversible past in his hands, and step out into the invincible future with him."

If you are struggling with addiction, anger or are easily offended, you have become comfortable with the uncomfortable and dysfunctional. You are flailing or failing in life, relationships, or vocation. You have found false comfort in the familiarity of destructive dynamics- to yourself and to your significant others.

If you are struggling with depression, anxiety and thoughts of self-loathing or suicide, the deceiver is stealing your joy and lying to you about who you are.

In either case, Jesus knows you and loves you as the person God created you to be. He made you on purpose for your individual purpose under God. Turn to Romans 8:28, God is love, self-love is self-discipline and the drive to the narrow gate of salvation and new life. YOU ARE WORTHY!

Matthew 7:7-8 "Ask *and it will be given to you; seek and you will find, knock and the door will be opened to you. For everyone who asks; receives, the one who seeks; finds, and to the one who knocks; the door will be opened.*"

Call a friend and build a support network today. Go to church. Pray to God. Speak to Jesus. Tell your family. Don't hold it in. You are not the only one. You are worthy. Self-discipline is self-love.

- **Mental health and addiction, call the SAMHSA National Hot line at**
  CALL 1-800-662-4357 or call your local mental health clinic.

- **For suicide and crisis, call/text the Suicide and Crisis hotline at**
  988/SMS 988 or 911

- **For drug, alcohol addiction, call the hotline for rehab at**
  1-844-924-2569

C.S. Lewis, author of "Mere Christianity," The Chronicles of Nardia" and many others: "You can't go back and change the beginning, but you can start where you are and change the ending."

Approximately ninety-three percent of suicide survivors are glad they did. We all make bad decisions in the throes of extreme emotions. Do not be shy to ask a sad person if they are ok. (Reference: 10 Things to Know from Those Who Have Attempted Suicide, by Sarah Klein, updated June 26, 2023. This was medically reviewed by Dakari Quimby, PhD).

SUICIDE IS SIN. An instrument of satan-the pimp of death. At funerals, people will say; "such a shame," or "a life wasted." Our God is a God of second chances. Never give up. Fight the good fight. Do not be shy to ask for help. You might save someone else's life one day.

(play *"Hold On"* by Katy Nichole, official music video).

Recommended: Boundless on K-Love on Demand, or Google Search *"Artist and author Tasha Layton invites you on a journey toward spiritual and emotional healing from the past hurts."*

1 Timothy 1:15 *"Here is a trustworthy saying that deserves full acceptance: Christ Jesus came into the world to save sinners of whom I am the worst."* There is both good and bad in most all individuals and groups with a variable balance in most all except our Lord and Savior Jesus Christ, who though perfect, does not expect and demand perfection in us. Amazing Grace! Can we, in our love and appreciation for Jesus just work on more consistency in being the best possible versions of ourselves-under God? Love God. Love others. Love you.

(play *"Christ in Me"* by, Jeremy Camp).

In 1 Timothy 1:18 The apostle Paul charged Timothy to "*fight the battle well*". What battle? The ageless battle between good and evil, externally, and internally. Each of us has our own battles; our own demons, or elements of our past we would like to forget, or that we struggle with or have swept under the rug of shame. Pull up the rug! Let go and let God!

But hey, as a Clinical Social Worker, I say to you as a fellow member of the fallible human race:

"Let's Do This Together!"

Say the following with me:

A: I admit that I am a sinner and have fallen short of God's goodness

B: I believe that Jesus died for my sins

C: I confess that Jesus is Lord of my life and is my Savior

Now pray this prayer:

"Take my shame; that I may live in the kingdom and be at peace in the love of the Father, the Son, and the Holy Spirit of Heaven. Thank you, Jesus. Amen."

Instructions for worship

1 Timothy 2:1-15 *"I urge then first that petitions, prayers, intercessions and thanksgiving be made for all people. For kings and all those in authority, that we may live peaceful and quiet lives in all godliness and holiness. This is good and pleases our God and Savior who wants all people to be saved and to come to the knowledge of the truth. For there is one God and one mediator between God and mankind, the man Christ Jesus."*

Qualifications for Overseers and Deacons

1 Timothy 3:1-9 *"Here is a trustworthy saying, whoever aspires to be an overseer desires a noble task. Now the overseer is to be above reproach (blame or disgrace), faithful to his wife, temperate, self-controlled, respectable, hospitable, able to teach, not given to drunkenness, not violent but gentle, not quarrelsome, not a lover of money. He must manage his own family well and see that his children obey him and must do so in a manner worthy of full respect. He must not be a recent convert, or he may become conceited and fall under the same judgment as the devil. He must keep hold of the deep truths of the faith with clear conscience."*

We should live our gospel beliefs and back them up with Jesus' worthy words and behaviors both in the church, at home and in the community.

Reasons for Paul's Instructions

Paul wrote his letters to young Timothy not knowing when or if he would live to rejoin him in person and knowing that new believers would need continued instructions and encouragement to persevere in their faith and gracious conduct under the pressures of temptations, false teachings, and persecution.

1 Timothy 3:15 *"If I am delayed, you will know how people ought to conduct themselves in God's household, which is the Church of the Living God, the pillar and foundation of the truth."*

1 Timothy 4:1-8 *"The spirit clearly says that in later times some will abandon the faith and follow deceiving spirits and things taught by demons. Have nothing to do with godless myths and old wives' tales, rather train yourself to be Godly. For physical training is of some value, but godliness has value for all things holding promise for both the present life and the life to come."*

Who else but a demon would lie, steal, cheat to win, scam the elderly, assault, murder and advocate death by abortion of a viable fetus developed enough to be comforted by the sound of his or her mother's voice?

False Teachers and Love of Money

Paul reminds the next and consecutive generations of followers to beware of the temptations of false teachings, and unhealthy interest in controversies, quarrels, envy, malice, corruption, and the distractions of the material world.

1 Timothy 6:5-7 *"Constant friction between people of corrupt minds, who have been robbed of the truth and who think that godliness is a means to financial gain. But godliness with contentment is a great gain. For we brought nothing into the world, and we take nothing out of it."*

But if we make idols of money and material gain, we miss out on the joy of giving.

> (play *"Material Girl"* by Madonna, official video).
> (just have fun with this one, no offense to Madonna)

In Acts 20 chapter 2 Paul had just bid farewell to the Ephesian Elders knowing he would be arrested in Jerusalem.

Acts 20:19 *"I served the Lord with great humility and with tears and in the midst of server testing by the ploys of my opponents."*

Acts 20:22-32 *"And now, compelled by the spirit, I am going to Jerusalem, not knowing what will happen to me there. Keep watch over yourselves and all flock of which the Holy Spirit has made you overseers. Be shepherds of the church of God. Now I am committing you to God and to the word of his grace, which can build you up and*

give you an instant inheritance among all those who are sanctified."
(Sanctified means to be set apart for special purpose or good works:
a holy purpose. It includes a change of heart and a desire to Love
God. Love People.)

(play *"Love God-Love People"* by, Danny Gokey).

Acts 20:35 *"In everything I did, I showed you that by this kind of hard
work we must help the weak, remembering the words the Lord Jesus
himself said, 'It is more blessed to give than to receive'."*

Final Charge to Timothy

Timothy 6:11-12 *"But you -Man of God- flee from all this, and pursue
righteousness, godliness, faith, love, endurance, and gentleness. Fight
the good fight of the faith. Command those who are rich in this present
world not to be arrogant, nor put their hope in wealth, which is so
uncertain., but to put their hope in God, who richly provides us with
everything for our enjoyment.*

*Command them to do good, to be rich in good deeds, and to be generous
and willing to share. In this way they will lay up treasures for themselves
as a firm foundation for the coming age, so that they may take hold of
the life that is truly life.*

*Timothy, guard what has been entrusted to your care. Turn away from
godless chatter and the opposing ideas of what is falsely called knowledge,
which some have professed and in so doing have departed from the faith.*

Grace be with you all"

(play *"The King is Alive"* by, Jordan Feliz, with lyrics
2023).

CHAPTER 11

Thanksgiving. Appeal for Loyalty. Appeal Renewed. False Teachings and Paul's Farewell Charge to Paster Timothy in 2 Timothy

Purpose: To give final instructions and encouragement to Timothy, Pastor of the Church is Ephesians.

Key Verse: *"Do your best to present yourself to God as one approved, a worker who does not need to be ashamed and who correctly handles the word of the truth."* (2:15)

Paul would soon be back in prison knowing he would be facing death. His condition was terminal. He was a convict, found guilty of following Jesus of Nazareth, who had previously been convicted in the court of the public opinion, having also been propagandized, slandered, and cancelled by the power brokers and talking heads of the times. Ecclesiastes 1:9 "… and there is nothing new under the sun."

When Paul arrived at the temple in Jerusalem, he was assaulted by fellow Jews for taking a Christian Gentile too far into the temple precincts. They had been lied to about Paul's intentions. Ironically, it was Roman soldiers that saved his life and a Roman captain who allowed Paul the opportunity to share his TRANSFORMATION story and testimony to the Jews who had attacked him.

Paul was often cut off from the world. He was a political prisoner, and, at this point, was jailed in Caesarea for two years and yet left with the instruments of writing and the time in isolation to continue his missionary penmanship at a pace that defied the dirty work of the false teachers and demons of the darkness. Faith and the pen is mightier than the sword!

And it is written in John 1:4-5 *"In the beginning was the word, and the word was with God, and the word was God. In him was life and that life was the light of all mankind. The light shines in the darkness, and the darkness has not overcome it."* We are the light of Today.

(play *"This Little Light of Mine"* by, Listener Kids, YouTube March 22, 2016).

1. Foundations of Christian Service (Life Application Study Bible)
2. Timothy 1 Paul, an apostle of Christ Jesus by the will of God, in keeping with the promise of life that is in Christ Jesus.

"To Timothy, my dear son: Grace, mercy, and peace from God the Father and Christ Jesus our Lord." (2)

Thanksgiving

"I thank God, whom I serve as my ancestors did, with a clear conscious, as night and day, I constantly remember you in my prayers. (3) I am reminded of your sincere faith, which first lived in your grandmother, Lois, and your mother, Eunice, and I am persuaded now lives in you also." (5).

Appeal for Loyalty

2 Timothy 1:6 *"For this reason, I remind you to fan into the flame, the gift of God, which is in you through the laying of hands. For the spirit of God gave us, does not make us timid, but gives us power, love, and self-discipline. So do not be ashamed of the testimony about our Lord or his prisoner. Rather, join me in suffering for the Gospel by the power of God. HE has saved us and called us to a holy life."*

Paul continues to drive home the challenge of paying the message of the Gospel forward. The tradition of and for the ages: Genesis 1:1 The Beginning. (3) God said, *"let there be light."*

2 Corinthians 3:15-18 Even to this day when Moses is read, a veil covers their hearts. *"But whenever anyone turns to the Lord, the veil is taken away. Now the Lord is the spirt and where the spirt of the Lord is, there is freedom. And we all, who with unveiled faces; contemplate the Lord's glory; are being TRANSFORMED into his image with ever-increasing glory, which comes from the Lord, who is the Spirit."*

2 Timothy 1:14 To Pastor Tim *"Guard the good deposit that was entrusted to you-guard it with the help of the Holy Spirt that lives in us."*

Appeal Renewed

2 Timothy 2:1-26 *"You then, my son, be strong in the grace that is in Christ Jesus"*. Paul appeals to Paster Tim to *"entrust the gospel to reliable people who will also be qualified to teach others."*

Concerns about false teachers, godless chatter, confusion about resurrection and wickedness bear repetition. Paul reminds us to remind others 22"Flee *the desires of youth and pursue righteousness, faith, love, and peace along with all those who call on the Lord out of a pure heart." 25" Opponents must be gently instructed in the hope that God will grant them repentance leading them to knowledge of the truth and that they will come to their senses and escape from the trap of the devil. (2:26)."*

Repentance is more than prayer for forgiveness of sins, but a deliberate and sincere change of mind regarding sin habits and impulses. Genuine repentance brings a change of direction in life, attitudes, and behaviors that can heal relationships, bring spiritual and financial stability and redemption (deliverance from the bondage of sin by the sacrifice of Jesus and the grace of God).

John 3:16 *"For God so loved the world that he gave his one and only son, so that whoever believes in him shall not perish but have eternal life."*

Acts 2:38 *"Repent and be baptized every one of you in the name of Jesus Christ for the forgiveness of your sins and you will receive the gift of the Holy Spirit."*

Read Galatians 5:22-23, The Fruit of the Spirit, then add to that the manifest power of goodness, the love of Jesus, wisdom and understanding, knowledge and counsel, fortitude and piety, a healthy fear of God, grace, mercy, forgiveness, restoration, sobriety, purpose hope, faith, and more peace.

2 Timothy 3:1 *"But they will not get very far because as in the case of those men, their folly will be clear to everyone."*

Paul's Final Charge to Timothy

Timothy 3:10-11 *"You, however, know all about my teaching, my way of life, my purpose, faith, patience, love, endurance, persecutions, sufferings; yet the Lord rescued me from all of them."*

Paul advised "evil doers and imposters will go from bad to worse, deceiving and being deceived." There is no honor amongst thieves.

Timothy 3:14 *"But as for you, continue in what you have learned and have been convinced of, because you know that from whom you learned it."*

Timothy 3:16-17 *"All scripture is GOD-breathed and is useful for teaching, rebuking, correcting, and training in righteousness, so that the servant of God may be thoroughly equipped for every good work."*

Play "Soul of Fire" by, Third Day, official lyric video).

CHAPTER 12

Appointing Elders for Goodness. Rebuke the Corrupt. Doing Good for the Sake of the Gospel. Saved to do Good. Final Remarks in Titus

---

Purpose: *"To advise Titus in his responsibility of supervising the churches on the Island of Crete."*

Paul was as strong a leader as he could be in service to Jesus Christ who was sent by our Holy Father to demonstrate the power of love for the blessings to serve others.

People flocked to hear Paul preach and teach. Great leaders eventually go on to their reward and their flocks may not be so receptive to their successors. But gospel is not about personalities and person appeal.

Different leaders come with different perspectives, experiences, and styles. Only God and his word stays the same. The job of pastors, priests, and ministers is not to be a crutch or idols to us. Thy are anointed spiritual leaders, encouragers, teachers, and most importantly faithful bearers of the gospel tradition; consistent in God's word, love, and good intentions for we- his obedient children.

When the new leader arrives, there should be no controversy or comparisons when the foundational rock and cornerstone of the Holy Trinity is understood and appreciated as the ultimate, uncompromising, incorruptible, and inextinguishable light of Jesus.

Key Verse: "The reason I left you in Crete was that you might put in order what was left unfinished and appoint elders in every town, as I directed you," (Timothy 1-5). Titus was a Greek believer, and like Timothy; was one of Paul's trusted missionary companions and close friends. The passion in Paul's letters of encouragement to the various churches in the world of the New Testament was in the redemption of his TRANSFOMATION and his epiphany on the road to Damascus; when Saul of Tarsus assimilated the passion of Christ, who saved him in a most dramatic style.

1 Leadership in the church (Life Application Study Bible)

Titus 1 *"Paul, a servant of God and an apostle of Jesus Christ to further the faith of God's elect and their knowledge of the truth that leads to godliness in the hope of eternal life, which God, who does not lie, promised from the beginning of time, (3) and which now at his appointed season he has brought to light through the preaching entrusted to me by the command of God our Savior."*

"To Titus, my true son, in our common faith; Grace and peace from God the Father and Christ Jesus our Savior." (4)

Appointing Elders Who Love What is Good

In Titus 1:5-9, Paul gives his good friend words of encouragement and a vote of confidence that he is worthy of his trust and capable of finishing what they started in Crete. Paul also shares his message in 1 Timothy as a reminder of the qualifications of church leaders in terms of behavior, temperament, integrity, and the ability to discern those same qualities in his inevitable successors.

Paul is our eternal guardian of the gospel and the mission to promote love, joy, peace, patience, goodness, kindness, gentleness, faithfulness, and self-control.

Titus 1:9 *"He must hold firmly to the trustworthy message* (as it has been taught), *so that he can encourage others by sound doctrine and refute those who oppose it."* (play *"For the Good"* by, Riley Clemming, lyrics video).

Rebuking Those Who Fail to do Good.

Titus 1:10 *"For there are many rebellious people, full of meaningless talk and deception, especially those of the circumcision group."* Recall in Galatians 2:11-14 the contentious rift between Paul and Peter over forcing adult gentile believers to follow Jewish law requiring circumcision as requirement of salvation.

In Galatians 2:21 Paul speaks to us *"I do not nullify the grace of God, for if righteousness comes through the law, then Christ died needlessly."*

Ephesian 2: 8-9 *"For it is by grace you have been saved, through faith and this not from yourselves, it is the gift from God; not as a result of works, so that none can boast."*

Christians are not perfect. No human is perfect. We are born innocent but grow into the world. We are susceptible to envy, gluttony, greed, lust, pride, sloth, and wrath. These are the seven deadly sins or cardinal sins in Christian teachings (Christian means "of Christ").

Some of the early Jewish believers were not all that welcoming to the individuals or groups considered outsiders. Paul recognized this and rebuked them.

Titus 1:12 *"One of Crete's own prophets has said it, Cretan's are always liars, evil brutes, lazy gluttons, therefore, rebuke them."*

Titus 1:16 *"They claim to know God, but by their actions they deny him. They are detestable, disobedient, and unfit for doing anything good."*

I try to avoid absolutes like always or never, because they are usually exaggerations in an otherwise weak argument or motivated by a sin trait. We all fall behind Jesus. We all leak and require a refilling of the Holy Spirit, by prayer and petition or self-examination. **What would Jesus do?** We all need a daily booster shot of prayer and thanksgiving for God's love, grace, and redemption. The intentional daily practice of giving thanks, expressing my gratitude and study of affirmations; is medicine without side effects.

Doing Good for the Sake of Gospel

Titus 2:1-2 *"You, however, must teach what is appropriate to sound doctrine. Teach the older men to be temperate, worthy of respect, self-controlled and sound in faith in love and in endurance."*

Galatians 5:22-23 *"But the fruit of the spirit is love, joy, peace, patience, goodness, kindness, gentleness, faithfulness and self-control."*

We tell the men in parish prisons; you might see clearly that love, joy, peace, patience, goodness, kindness, and gentleness are blessings to receive and pay forward. But you might not be so sure about faithfulness and self-control. Some of us do not like being told what to do. But take heart in faithfulness and self-control. These are what make possible any goodness that comes from God who is the spirit and Jesus who is Lord of our new lives in Christ. Amen.

Titus 2:11 *"For the Grace of God has appeared that offers salvation to all people. IT teaches us to say 'no' to ungodliness and worldly passions, and to live self-controlled, upright, and godly lives in this present age."*

And Jesus reminds us in John 14:1 *"Let not your heart be troubled. You believe in God; believe also in me."*

John 14:6 *"I am the way and the truth and the life."*

Ecclesiastes 1:9 *"What has been, will be again, what has been done will be done again, there is nothing new under the sun."*

John 16:33 *"I have told you these things, so that in me you may have peace. In this world you will have trouble. But take heart for I have overcome the world."*

Saved In Order to Do Good

In Titus 3, The Apostle Paul is speaking to us about right living in society. This includes obedience to God's law to love others as our default position. We are to avoid judgment of others based on small samples of knowledge.

Matthew 7:1 *"Do not be judged, or you too will be judged."* We are to operate in humility and gentleness. Humility means to have an accurate estimate of our abilities as well as our limitations. We honor God in all humility.

Right living in society also means living in obedience to laws legally passed by our representatives in Congress. Our great constitution wisely includes system of checks and balances that America's founding fathers devised, under God, to combat the corruption they knew would eventually creep into the soul of the greatest land on the planet.

Titus 3:1 *"Remind the people to be subject to the rulers and authorities, to be obedient, to be ready to do whatever is good."* By God's enteral standards or vote them out!

Paul reminds us of the foolish ways we lived in obedience to "all kinds of passions and pleasures."

Titus 3:4-5 *"But when the kindness and love of God our savior appeared, he saved us, not because of the righteous things we done, but because of his mercy. He saved us through the washing of rebirth and renewal by the Holy Spirit generously through Jesus."*

Final Remarks

Titus 3:14 *"Our people must learn to devote themselves to doing what is good in order to provide for urgent needs and not live unproductive lives."*

The letters of Timothy and Titus were Paul's last and mark the end of his public ministry. Paul's devotion to Jesus, the Kingdom of God, we his chosen and peace on earth resonates in his last and eternal hoorah of encouragement for new leaders and all keepers of the faith.

We will close out the Pauline Epistles with what was to be a private and personal letter about slavery-literal and metaphoric and a "small masterpiece of grace, tact and a profound demonstration of true Christian fellowship in action and the power of Christ to unite those separated by barriers." (Life Application Study Bible)

(play *"Desert Road,"* by Casting Crowns, official
music video)

CHAPTER 13

Thanksgiving. Paul's Plea for Grace and Inclusion in Philemon

This is a private and personal letter to a friend, written in AD 60, during Paul's first imprisonment in Rome. Paul's friend, Philemon, was a wealthy member of the Colossian Church.

Purpose: To convince Philemon to forgive his runaway slave, Oneimus, and to accept him as a brother in the faith.

Setting: Slavery was very common in the Roman Empire, and even some Christians had slaves. While Paul does not condemn slavery in his writings, he makes a radical statement by calling Onesimus Philemon's brother in Christ.

Key Verse: "Perhaps the reason he was separated from you for a little while was that you might have him back forever. -no longer as a slave, but better than a slave, as a dear brother. He is very dear to me, but even dearer to you, both as a fellow man and as a brother in the Lord.

1 Paul's appreciation for Philemon (Life Application Study Bible)

"Paul, a prisoner of Christ Jesus and Timothy's brother,

to Philemon our dear friend and fellow worker- also to Apphia our sister and Archippus our fellow soldier- and to the church that meets in your home.

Grace and peace to you from God our Father and the Lord Jesus Christ."

Thanksgiving and Prayer

4 *"I always thank God as I remember you in my prayers, because I hear about your love for all his holy people and your faith in the Lord Jesus. I pray that your partnership with us in the faith effective in deepening your understanding of every good thing we share for the sake of Christ. Your love has given me great joy and encouragement, because you, brother, have refreshed the hearts of the Lord's people."*

Paul was preparing Philemon for a big ask-to forgive and welcome home his slave, Onesimus who had stolen from him and run away to Rome where he met Paul. Paul Transformed Onesimus to a believing follower of Jesus and so saved him, just as he had done for Philemon and much earlier experienced for himself in dramatic fashion on the road to Damascus-by Jesus Christ personally!

Paul's Plea for Onesimus

Philemon 8 *"Therefore, although in Christ I could be bold and order you to do what you ought to do, yet I prefer to appeal to you on the basis of love...that I appeal to you for my son, Onesimus, who became my son while I was in chains."*

Slavery was common in ancient times but different from the slavery we are familiar with in the western world around the time of colonization and in the growing pains of the baby named Democracy, born in the United States of America, circa 1776. America, God's country, had freed its citizens from the tyranny of the totalitarian state and had to grow into the promise of The Declaration of Independence, which was laid upon the cornerstone of Jesus and continued in his disciples, that all men (all human beings), are created equal from the throne of love in heaven above. From the beginning- "God is Love."

In the world of Philemon and Paul, and upon conversion to Christian fellowship, Onesimus was elevated out of slavery and automatically injected into the status of equal importance in the Body of Christ, with all rights, responsibilities and Heavenly expectations. Can I get an Amen?

Parenthetically, all deliberate Christians, are freed and liberated from the bondage of sin, and in modern times, emancipated from the abomination of literal human bondage. Man's inhumanity to mankind. Christianity is the power of God's love and the potential of our servant hearts and governing bodies to set things right.

Philemon 15-16 *"Perhaps the reason he was separated from you for a little while was that you might have him back forever- no longer a slave, but better than a slave, as a dear brother. He is very dear to me, but even dearer to you, both as a fellow man, and as a brother in the Lord."*

Paul reminds us of the mission of the kingdom of God and we are the workers on this mission trip. We are overcoming the destruction of sin that separated us from God and so each other. We are in the process of discovering Jesus' power over the sin nature in us and the realization of our true kingdom purpose under the Father, through the Son and with the in-dwelling Holy Spirit of Truth. We are learning the power of love in unity and diversity in the Body of Christ.

The Apostle Paul had no fear of suffering or death. He preached joy in all circumstances, intimacy in Christian Relationships and the intimacy of discipleship. He teaches us that peace lies in the power of grace and forgiveness. He reminds us to have faith in Jesus for eternal life and justice. He reminds us that the healing power of the Holy Spirit is within us, that we are God's chosen and adopted children and heirs to his Kingdom. Paul nudges us into agreement with the beauty of unity in diversity, and that we need to seek salvation in the death of our old selves to have a new life in Jesus and our servant hearts. And most importantly, Paul wants to guide us into love as our default position in our human encounters with both angels and sinners.

(play *"I'm So Blessed"* by, Cain, lyrics).

SECTION 7

The Post Pauline Epistles and John's Revelation

CHAPTER 1

The Sufficiency and Supremacy of Jesus in the Book of Hebrews

Purpose: To present the sufficiency and superiority of Jesus.

Author: Unknown

Original Audience: Hebrew Christians, drifting back to the familiarity of Old Testament Judaism; some in fear of persecution, some with an immature understanding of Christ's sovereign authority and identity as God.

Date Written: Most likely before the destruction of the Temple in Jerusalem in AD70, that Christ predicted in the Olivet Discourse: Jesus' extended teaching to his disciples on the Mount of Olives.

Key Verse: "The Son is the radiance of God's glory and exact representation of his being, sustaining all things by his powerful word. After he had provided purification for sins, he sat down at the right hand of the majesty in heaven." (1:3)

6 Mega Themes

1. Christ as superior
2. Christ's sacrifice
3. The High Priest
4. Maturity
5. Faith
6. Endurance

Mega Theme 1. Christ as Superior

Hebrews 1:1-3 *"In the past God spoke to our ancestors through the Prophets at many times and in various ways. But in these last days, he has spoken to us by his son, whom he appointed heir of all things and through whom also he made the universe. The Son is the radiance of God's glory and the exact representation of his being, sustaining all things, by his powerful word."*

In John 1: *God's word came to the world and became flesh. (1:4) "In him was life, and that life was the light of all mankind."*

John 1:1 *"The word became flesh and made his dwelling among us, have seen his glory, from the Father, full of grace and truth."*

Hebrews 1:3-4 (continued), *"After he had provided purification for shins, he sat down at the right hand of the majesty in heaven. So, he became as much as superior to the angels as the name he has inherited is superior to theirs."*

Hebrews 2:1-3 *"We must pay the most careful attention, therefore, to what we have heard, so that we don't drift away. For since the message spoken through angels was binding and every violation and disobedience received its punishment, how shall we escape if we ignore so great a salvation?"*

So, this unnamed author, likely a disciple, or a close associate, was concerned for believers who were drifting back to Old Testament doctrine and so away from the salvation and peace we have found in serving Jesus. In the dark world of addictions, people getting sober tend to drift back into their old ways of coping with the world because those ways are familiar. Familiarity in false needs and immediate gratification is false comfort.

Mega Themes 2 Christ's Sacrifice, 3 The High Priest, and 4 Maturity

Hebrews 2:14 *"Since the children have flesh and blood, he too shared in their humanity so that by his death he might break to power of him who holds the power of death that's in the devil."*

Hebrew 2:16-17 *"For surely it is not the angels he helps but Abrahams' descendants. For this reason, he had to be made like them that he might become a merciful and faithful High Priest in service to God, and that he might make atonement for the sins of the people."*

Hebrews 4:15 *"For we do not have a high priest who is unable to empathize with our weaknesses; be we have one who has been tempted in every way yet did not sin. Let us then approach God's throne of grace with confidence, so that we may receive mercy and find grace to help us in our time of need."*

Hebrews 6:1 *"Therefore let us move beyond the elementary teachings about Christ and be taken forward to maturity."*

Hebrews 6:4-6 *"For those...who have once been enlightened and who have fallen away to be brought back into repentance."*

Hebrews 7:24-25 *"But because Jesus lives forever, he has a permanent priesthood. Therefore, he is able to save completely those who came to God through him, because he lives to intercede for them."*

Hebrews 7:27 *"Unlike other high priests, he does not need to offer sacrifices day after day...he sacrificed for their sins once and for all when he offered himself."*

Mega Theme 3 The High Priest of New Covenant

Hebrews 8:1-2 *"Now the main point of what we are saying is this: we do have such a High Priest, who serves in the sanctuary, the true tabernacle, set up by the Lord, not by a mere human being."*

Hebrews 8:5-6 *"They (the Levite Priests) serve at a sanctuary that is a copy and a shadow of what is in heaven. But in fact, the ministry Jesus has received is as superior to theirs as the covenant of which he is mediator, is superior to the old one, since the new covenant is established on better promises."*

Under the old Jewish system, only those from the tribe of Levi were allowed to be priests. Jesus, from the tribe of Judah would have been excluded.

Mega Theme 2 Christ's Sacrifice- Once and for All

Hebrews 9:27-28 *"Just as people are destined to die once and after that face judgement, so Christ was sacrificed once to take away the sins of many; and he will appear a second time, not to bear sin, but to bring salvation to those who are waiting for him."*

Yet another prophesy of Revelation-the second coming of Jesus.

Mega Theme 2 (continued): Christ's Sacrifice-Once for All

Hebrews 10:4-7 *"It is impossible for the blood of bulls and goats to take away sins. Therefore, when Christ came into the world, he said* 'sacrifice and offerings you did not desire, but a body you prepared for me; with burnt offerings and sin offerings you were not pleased.' Then I said, 'Here I am-it is written about me in the scroll-I have come to do your will, my God.'"

The Levite Priests, I am sure were seriously devout believers in God and deeply knowledgeable of the law and process of officiating over ritual sin offerings.

But the New Covenant established that one sacrifice was to be made once and for all time, based on one word, that was born of an inextinguishable light when God's word became flesh. That word is love, for God so loved the world.

> (play *"Child of God"* by, Crowder, Austin City
> Limits Live 2022).

Hebrews 10:12-14 *"But when this priest had offered for all time one sacrifice for sins, he sat down at the right hand of God, and since that time he waits for his enemies to be made his footstool. For by one sacrifice, he has made perfect forever those who are being made holy."* (us)

Hebrews 10:18 *"And where these sins have been forgiven, sacrifice for sin is no longer necessary."*

Mega Themes 5 Faith, and 6 Endurance in Encouragement

Hebrews 10:19-22 *"Therefore, brothers and sisters, since we have confidence to enter the most holy place by the blood of Jesus, by a new and living way opened for us through the curtain, that is his body, and since we have a great priest over the house of God, let us draw near to God with a sincere heart and with the full assurance that faith brings."*

Hebrews 10:24-25 *"And let us consider how we may spur one another on toward love and good deeds, not giving up meeting together, but encouraging one another."*

Hebrews 10:32 "Remember those earlier days after you had received the light, when you endured in a great conflict full of suffering."

Hebrews 10:36 *"You need to persevere so that when you have done the will of God, you will receive what he has promised."*

Enduring times of chaos, tyranny, and covid, let us not be consumed in worry or defeated in fear of any political faction or deceiver on earth, but encouraged in the faith in and knowledge of the permanent High Priest of the Kingdom who is here now, yesterday, tomorrow, and eternally.

Faith in Action

Hebrews 11:1-3 *"Now faith is confidence in what we hope for and assurance about what we don't see. This is what the ancients were commended for. By faith, we understand that the universe was formed at God's command, so that what is seen was not made out of what was visible."*

By faith, the heroes of the Bible endured and persevered. (See the heroes listed in Hebrews 17.) Modern Christian brothers and sisters who dwell under the totalitarian thumb of many countries around the world still do. Regarding our just signed and God blessed Constitution in 1776, a lady asked Ben Franklin if we have a republic or a monarchy-Doctor Franklin replied, "A republic, if you can keep it."

Hebrews 12:1 *"Therefore, since we are surrounded by such a great crowd of witnesses, let us throw off everything that hinders and the sin that so easily entangles. And let us run with perseverance the race marked out for us."*

Hebrews 13:1 *"Keep loving one another as brothers and sisters. Do not forget to show hospitality to strangers, for by doing, some people have shown hospitality to angels without knowing it. Continue to remember people in prison as if you were together with them in prison, and those who are mistreated as if you yourselves were suffering."*

Amazing Empathy- Amazing Grace

We give thanks for the Superior Empathy of Christ's sacrifice, his permanent High Priesthood of salvation, the maturity of the Body of Christ, and the perfect faith of Jesus' endurance to the death that we may have New Life and fear, no more.

(play *"Fear No More"* by building forty-nine, lyrics)

CHAPTER 2

Trails and Temptations. Listening and Doing. Favoritism Forbidden. Faith and Deeds. Taming the Tongue. Two kinds of Wisdom. Submission to God and a Warning to Rich Oppressors in the Book of James.

Purpose: To expose hypocritical practices and to teach how Christians should live.

Author: James, Jesus' brother, and a leader in the Jerusalem church.

Original Audience: First century Christians residing in Gentile communities outside of Judea.

Key Verse: "But someone will say, 'you have faith; I have deeds, show me your faith without deeds, and I will show you my faith by my deeds." (2:18)

1 Genuine Religion (Life Application Study Bible)

James 1:1 James a servant of God and the Lord Jesus Christ, to the twelve tribes scattered among the nations: Greetings. After Stephen was martyred (stoned to death) in Acts 7:54, with Saul of Tarsus looking on -persecutions increased and Christians in Jerusalem were scattered throughout the Roman world.

Trials and Tribulations

James 1:2-3 *"Consider it pure joy, by brothers and sisters, whenever you face trails of many kinds. Because you know that they are testing of your faith produces perseverance under trail because having stood the test, that person will receive the crown of life that the Lord has promised to those who love him."*

Listening and Doing

James 1:19-20 *"Everyone should be quick to listen, slow to speak and slow to anger. Because human anger does not produce the righteousness that God desires."*

Proverbs 16:32 *"He who is slow to anger, that ruleth his spirit is stronger than he who conquers a city."*

James 1:22 *"Do not merely listen to the word, and so deceive yourself. Do what it says."*

Faith and deeds

James 2:14 *"What good is it, my brothers, and sisters if someone claims to have faith but has no deeds? Can faith save them?"*

Ephesians 2:8-9 *"For it is by grace that you have been saved, through faith- and this is not from yourselves, it is the gift of God. Not by works, so that no one can boast."*

James 2:16-17 *"If one of you says to them, 'go in peace, keep warm and well fed', but does nothing more. What good is it? In the same way, faith by itself if it is not accompanied by action, is dead."*

Well wishes and pleasantries are small, but significant blessings if sincerely spoken, but at some point, in our maturation as deliberate Christians, we will notice a growing tendency to feel and act upon the grace of God and love of Jesus.

We will by deliberate actions or random opportunities, in our servant hearts; perceive and receive family, friends, acquaintances and strangers as Children of God consistently. No longer just a means to an end or mere cogs in a machine; but each a CHILD of GOD " in the human wheel of fortune. We will know God well enough to break the chains of complacency, walk in kingdom purpose and find joy in making a difference even if it is only to call the cashier, clerk, or server by their name. Jesus calls his Disciples BY Our NAME! Get ready for the smile of a recognized soul!

Favor Forbidden

James 2:1 *"My brothers and sisters, believers in our glorious Lord Jesus Christ must not show favoritism."*

James 2:5 *"Has not God chosen those who are poor in the eyes of the world to be rich in faith and to inherit the Kingdom he promised to those who love him?"* James reminds us of the Greatest Commandment- "love your neighbors as yourself." 6" But you have dishonored the poor. Is it not the rich who are exploiting you? 8 "If you keep the royal law found in scripture, 'Love your neighbor as yourself' you are doing right. 9 But if you show favoritism, you sin and are convicted by the law as lawbreakers."

In Philippians 52:2-6 Paul agrees *"In your relationships with one another, have the same mindset as Christ Jesus who being in very nature God, did not consider equality with God something to be used to his own advantage."* God's true greatness and any genuine goodness in me comes with humility. It is my pride that comes before my fall.

Submit Yourselves to God

James 4:1-3 *"What causes fights and quarrels among you? Don't they come from your desires that are battles within you? You desire but do not have, so you kill. You covet but you cannot get what you want, so you quarrel and fight."*

How often do we lie to ourselves when we think or say out loud "I need _____. I NEED IT!" Such a wanton lie; extravagant, unruly, undisciplined, sensual, lustful, or just plain greedy. I did not need a fifty-five-inch flat screen, streaming television. So, I got it. I did not discuss this substantial purchase with my wife or comprehend the sufficiency and supremacy of Jesus.

James 4:6-8 *"But he gives us more grace. That is why scripture says: God opposes the proud but shows favor to the humble. Submit yourselves, then to God. Resist the devil, and he will flee from you. Come near to God and he will come near to you."*

How often do our selfish tendencies and pride isolate us from our servant hearts and embolden the devil into our thoughts, desires and actions that are not under God, or of Jesus?

Philippians 4:6 *"Don't worry about anything; instead, pray about everything. Tell God what you need and thank him for all he has done."*

(play *"See Me Through It"* by, Brandon Heath, official lyric video.)

(play *"People Are Crazy"* by, Billy Currington, lyrics).

CHAPTER 3

Praise to God for Living Hope. Be holy. The Living Stone and Chosen People. Living Godly among pagans. Suffering from doing Good. Living for God. Suffering for being a Christian and Flock to the Elders in 1 Peter.

Purpose: To offer encouragement to suffering Christians

Original Audience: Christians scattered throughout the Roman Empire

Key Verse: *"These trails have come so that the proven genuineness of your faith may result in praise, glory and honor when Jesus Christ is revealed."* (1 Peter 1:7)

The persecution that began in Jerusalem spread to the rest of the known world, especially after Rome had decided and were determined to rid the Roman empire of the Christ-Ones" (those who would not bow to Caesar). The Jewish nation was eventually scattered to the four corners of the earth. Peter wrote to the church, the believers, and adherents to God's commandments of grace and love, to continue the message of salvation, peace, and new holy life in Jesus' name. Peter continues the tradition of Jesus and his disciples to encourage us in endurance, even in the darkest of circumstances.

This tradition of unbreakable cohesion of *"3,300 of the Jewish story"* (chabad.org); continues in the New Testament Christianity.

In all human history, with so many other civilizations reduced to archaeological relics among the Jewish culture and citizens, "No other people have survived for so long under the circumstances" (chabad.org/ article "The Science of Jewish Survival" by Dov Greenberg.

The Bible is more than a history of the 12 tribes of Israel. It is the never-ending story of Us in the bosom of the Father, the Son and the Holy Spirit; for ever and ever Amen.

Our salvation is a generous gift from God. We Gentiles are privileged (and blessed) to belong to God's family (A Jesus Christ Community. ..What a glorious sub division!).

1 God's great blessings to his people (Life Application Study Bible)

1 Peter 1: Peter, an Apostle of Jesus Christ, *"to God's elect, exiles scattered throughout the provinces of Pontus, Galatia, Cappadocia, Asia and Bithynia, who have been chosen according to the foreknowledge of God the Father, through the sanctifying work of the spirit to be obedient to Jesus Christ and sprinkled with his blood."*

By sanctification we are Washed Clean from sin, set apart and made fit for a Holy Purpose.

"Grace and peace by yours in abundance."

Praise to God for a Living Hope

1 Peter 1:3-4 *"Praise be to God and Father of our Lord Jesus Christ! In his great mercy he has given us new birth into a living hope through the resurrection of Jesus Christ from the dead, and into an inheritance that can never perish, spoil, or fade."*

1 Peter 1:6-9 *"In all this you greatly rejoice though now for a little while you may have to suffer grief in all kinds of trails. These have come so that the proven genuineness of your faith - of greater worth than gold, which perishes even though refined in fire - may result in praise, glory, and honor when Jesus Christ is revealed. Though you have not seen him, you love him, you believe in him and are filled with an inexpressible and glorious joy, for you are receiving the end results of your faith; the salvation of your souls."*

How many times have we said "WHY ME" in times of suffering, troubles, hardship, disappointment, struggles, grief, and loss? The real question is "WHY NOT ME"? What human being is immune from the imperfections and complications of life? Here is a true reliable statement: **Life is about 10% off what happens to us and 90% of how we respond to it.** How many of our wounds are self-inflicted? Life is uncertain. God is a love that remains in all circumstances. **Trails do not define us, they refine us.** We mere Christians will never be perfect, but as we grow in the strength of our maker, and the way of Jesus, we become the best possible versions of ourselves.

The supernatural perseverance of Jesus redefines us and blesses us with the character of hope in unity, with the contented and holy natured Paul and Peter of the original twelve disciples, because we are their descendants!

Be Holy

1 Peter 1:13-14 *"Therefore, with minds that are alert, and are fully sober, set your hope on the grace to be brought to you when Jesus Christ is revealed at his coming. As obedient children, do not conform to the evil desires you had when you lived in ignorance."*

"The Cry of the Soul" by Dr. Dan B. Allender and Dr. Tremper Longman, III.

"The Psalms helps us to embrace negative thoughts and emotions, to bring them to God. This is in contrast with the culture norms of man, which are to repress and discourage their expression. The Psalms voice "The Cry of the Soul," while acknowledging the hunger and hope of our souls."

Psalms 23:1-6 *"The Lord is my shepherd, I lack nothing..."*

"The Psalmist invites us to feel emotion without immediate resolution and urges us to live with hunger. But we are to succumb to neither pious happiness nor cynical disillusionment. (Psalm 3:3, Psalm 18:35 and Psalm 4:8).

The Psalmist attests that our God is a God who restores. (Psalms 34:18, and Psalms 113:7-9).

The goodness of God is mysterious and ironic in that the brings us to him through suffering to assuage our suffering(s)."

1 Peter 1:15-16 *"But just as he who called you is holy, so be holy in all you do. For it is written 'be holy, because I am holy.'"*

1 Peter 1:23 *"For you have been born again not of perishable seed, but imperishable, through the living and enduring word of God."*

1 Peter 2:1-3 *"Therefore, rid yourselves of all malice, and all deceit, hypocrisy, envy, and slander every kind. Like newborn babies, crave pure spiritual milk, so that by it you may grow up in your salvation, now that you have tasted that the Lord is good."*

(play *"First Things First"* by, Consumed by Fire, official lyric video)

Final Greetings

1 Peter 5:12 *"Peace to all of you who are in Christ."*

CHAPTER 4

Confirming one's Calling and Election. The Prophesy of Scripture. False Teachers and their Destruction on the Day of the Lord in Second Peter.

Purpose: To warn Christians about false teachers and to "exhort" (an urgent appeal, warning, or advice) them to grow in their faith in knowledge of Christ. (Written three years after First Peter. Likely in Rome).

Setting: Peter knew his time on earth was limited (1 Peter 1:13-14), so he wrote what was on his heart; warning believers of what would happen when he was gone, especially about the presence of false teachers. Peter reminds his readers of the unchanging word of God and the truth that Jesus said in John 8:31-32. "*To the Jews who had believed in him, 'if you hold to my teachings, you are really my disciples. Then you will k now the truth, and the truth will set you free.*"

BONUS STUDY: **Was Peter the First Pope?**

The Catholic tradition considers that the Catholic Church is the continuation of the early Christian community established by the disciples of Jesus. (Wikipedia.org) Most of the research I found; speaks of St. Peter as the Pope."

There is a question posed on study.com, for which there are several possible answers. *"All Popes were subjects to the Roman Empire, so no one can say that Saint Peter was the first Roman Pope."* Then, in the same article, "The first Pope, Peter," *led the early Christians and travelers to Rome."*

Then we remember the first time Jesus was introduced to Andrew's fellow fisherman and brother Simon, when Andrew exclaimed in John 1:41-42 "'we have found the Messiah', and we brought him to Jesus." *Jesus looked at him and said "you are Simon, son of John. You will be called Cephas."* Cephas means rock in Aramaic, and Petros, or Peter in the Greek translation (Jesus knew Peter). Peter acknowledged Jesus in Matthew 16:16-18, *You are the Messiah, the son of the living God. Jesus replied, 'blessed are you, Simon, son of Jonah, for this was not revealed to you by flesh and blood, but by my Father in heaven. And I tell you that you are Peter, and on this rock, I will build my church, and the Gates of Hades will not overcome it.'"*

John or Jonah? An article at cambridge.org speculates that near the end of his three-year ministry, Jesus may have cited the name of Jonah as the father of Simon Peter *"in order to distinguish him from the other Simon among the twelve."*

Key Verse: "His divine power has given us everything we need for a godly life through our knowledge of him who called us by his own glory and goodness." (1 Peter 1:3)

In Hosea 4 God had a charge against his chosen and beloved people. *"There is no faithfulness, no love, no acknowledgment of God in the land. There is only cursing, lying and murder, stealing and adultery. My people are destroyed from lack of knowledge."*

How sad.

Jesus and his disciples; then and still to this day, are vested in the wellbeing of travelers on this planet earth. The place on which God formed creatures in "their" image and with free will.

1 Guidance for Growing Christians (Life Application Study Bible)

2 Peter 1:1 Simon Peter, a servant and apostle of Jesus Christ. *"To those who through the righteousness of our Lord and Savior Jesus Christ have received faith as precious as ours. Grace and Peace be yours in abundance through the knowledge of God and of Jesus our Lord."*

Concerning One's Calling and Election

2 Peter 3-4 *"His divine power has given us everything we need for a godly life through our knowledge of him who called us by his own glory and goodness. Through these he has given us his very great and precious promises, so that through them you may participate in the divine nature, having escaped the corruption in the world caused by evil desires."*

(What are we willing to do, to strengthen ourselves against the lies and temptations of Satan and his minions who desperately wants to unsettle us from our divine promises?)

In Romans 5 *"Perseverance builds character and character builds hope."*

In 1 Corinthians 5 we expel the devil and gain the kingdom.

In 2 Corinthians 5 in Christ, we are a new creation and appointed as Christ's Ambassadors.

In Galatians 5 *"If we walk by the spirit and tame the flesh, we have the Fruit of the Spirit: Love, Joy, Peace, Patience, Kindness, Goodness, Gentleness, Faithfulness and Self Control."*

In Ephesians 5 *"We walk in the way of love, and the devil flees."*

In Philippians 2 Paul is full of joy if we think and love and live like Jesus.

In Colossians 3:23 *"Whatever you do, work it with all your heart and win the inheritance of the Lord Jesus."*

In 1 Thessalonians 1 and 5 endurance is inspired by our hope in Jesus. We encourage each other, build each other up and even give thanks in all circumstances.

In 2 Thessalonians we "stand firm and hold fast to the teachings" (and pay it forward).

In 1 Timothy, Paul urges, petitions, prayers, intercession, and thanksgiving be made for all people including those in authority; that we may live in peace, godliness and holiness that pleases God our Savior, (4) *"who wants all people to be saved and to come to a knowledge of the truth."*

In 2 Timothy, Paul reminds us to *"fan into flame the gift of God, which is in you through the laying on of hands. For the spirit of God gave us does not make us timid."*

In Titus, Paul says we are saved in order to do good.

The early church consisted of mostly small groups of fresh and devout believers, often meeting in private homes or in remote, safe places in fear of scorn from other Jews or persecution of the legal elites of those times.

PRESENT DAY SUNDAY SERVICE is a continuation of the preservation and growth of the faith in the Holy Trinity. Modern day small groups, bible studies and discipleship groups are more intimate versions of the experience of entering, the Sunday service sanctuary worship music, and Holy Spirit greetings.

SMALL GROUPS are where we get to know one another, and turbo charge the growth of the Body of Christ.

So, this is what we can do to strengthen our faith, lift our spirits, and overcome Satan's temptation when we walk the walk and talk the talk of Jesus on the narrow path to salvation. This is where we secure our reservations at the House of the Father, the Son the Holy Spirit, and our deeply departed.

Prophesy of Scripture

2 Peter 1:12-13 *"So I will always remind you of these things, even though you know them and are firmly established in the truth you now have. I think it is right to refresh your memory as long as I live in the tent of this body."*

Peter must have been reading my mind. I was just thinking about the rowdy ex-slaves on the road out of Egypt. How many times did they fall back into worship of Baal? How many times do we need Father God to slap our hands away from a hot stove?

Numbers 21:6-9 *"So the Lord sent them poisonous snakes; they bit the people and many Israelites died. The people came to Moses. They confessed their sins and plead 'take the snakes away from us.'"*

Numbers 21:8 The heavenly Father had love and mercy for his brats, *"the lord said to Moses make a snake and put it up on a pole and anyone who is bitten can look at it and live."*

In the modern medical community, the snake on the pole is a symbol of healing.

Baal (pronounced (bāle) is a name given to an image or multiple dieties, a false god or false teacher and a wooden idol that God commanded his people not to worship. It is correct to say our memories and our hearts need refreshment.

False Teachers and Their Destruction

2 Peter 2:1 *"But there were also false prophets among the people, just as there will be false teachers among you. They will secretly introduce destructive heresies, even enying the soverign Lord who baught t hem-bringing swift destruction to themselves."*

Jesus had told his disciples that false teachers would come contradicting the true prophets in the Old Testament; telling people only what they wanted to hear. The ignorant and the corrupt narcisists did and are, still twisting Christ's teaching and the words of the disciples.

Have you ever bought a product that looked really good on t.v. and received plastic junk in you mailbox? And what was the price? What sayeth the false prophet? "Only $19.99!"

2 Peter 2:12 *"But these people blastpheme in matters they do not understand. They are like unreasoning animals, creatures of instinct, born only to be caught and destroyed. And like animals, they too will parish."*

2 Peter 2:22 *"Of them the proverbs are true: "A dog returns to its own vomit, and a sow that is washed, returns to her wallowing in the mud."*

The Day of The Lord

2 Peter 3:1-3 *"Dear friends, this is now my second letter to you. I have written both of them as reminders to stimulate you to wholesome thinking. I want you to recall the words spoken in the past by the holy prophets and the command given by our Lord and Savior through your apostles. Above all, you must understand that in the last days, scoffers will come, scoffing, and following their own evil desires."*

Some among us think what they want to think, say what they want to say and do what they want to do. Amen?

In 2 Peter 2:5-7 Peter reminds us of things that the scoffers *"deliberately forget, that long ago by God's word the heavens came into being and the earth was formed out of water and by water. By these waters also the world of that time was deluged and destroyed. By that same word, the present heavens and earth are reserved for fire, being kept for the day of judgement and destruction of the ungodly."*

There is geologic and fossil evidence of a swift and violent global flood. *"The earth is scarred with evidence of the worldwide flood in Genesis." Global evidence of the Genesis Flood,"* article by Dr. Andrew A. Snelling on July 1, 2021, featured in Answers magazine.

2 Peter 3:10 *"But the day of the Lord will come like a thief. The heavens will disappear with a roar; the elements will be destroyed by fire and the earth, and everything done in it will be laid bare."13 But in keeping with his promise we are looking forward to a new heaven and a new earth, where righteousness dwells."*

Saint Peter, a representative of Jesus our Lord and ambassador to the Kingdom of Heaven wants us to prosper in the fruits of the spirit (Galatians 5:22), redemption, sanctification, justification, restoration, sobriety, purpose, hope and more peace.

2 Peter 3:18 *"But grow in the grace and knowledge of our Lord and savior Jesus Christ: to him be glory both now and forever! Amen."*

There is great peace in this prayer from Saint Peter, and peace in the humility of praise and worship and docile obedience to higher authority that lifts us up in love and encouragement.

> (play *"Fear is not my Future"* by, Maverick City Music).

CHAPTER 5

The Word of life. Light and Darkness. Love and Hatred. Reasons for Writing. Not Loving the World. You Know in the Son. God's children and sin. Denying the Incarnation. God's love and Ours. Faith in the Incarnate Son of God in I John

Purpose: To reassure Christians in their faith and to counter false teachings

Date Written: Likely between AD85 and AD90. As an eyewitness of Christ John wrote authoritatively giving a new generation of believers' assurance and confidence in Jesus and trust in their newfound faith in God, who was, and is, the higher authority over and above the ruling class lords of hypocrisy. (They had not yet exiled him to the island of Patmos).

Key Verse: "I write these things to you who believe in the name of the Son of God so that you may know that you have eternal life." (5:3).

As an elder statesman in the church, John wrote this letter to his dear children and presents God as "light, love, and life. "And yet most of us recall the indiscretions and passions of a rowdy youth not always well spent. John and his brother James were among first disciples called by Jesus who quickly recognized their bold and aggressive personalities. He called them out in Mark 3:17 as Boanergēs "Sons of Thunder."

In Luke 9:51-55 *"When Jesus was not welcomed at a Samaritan village, the young rowdies asked Jesus 'Lord, do you want us to call fire down from heaven and destroy them?' But Jesus turned and rebuked them. Then he and his disciples went to another village."*

As we mellow with age, wisdom, and knowledge, we find peace and confidence in Jesus. Our passion and zeal to testify for the Kingdom of Heaven remains as our thoughts and words are seasoned more with honey than salt. And more light than vinegar. Jesus had little time on earth to waste on drama.....and yet he bore it.

John, James, and fellow rowdy and Saint-to-be Peter found their purpose, method, and confidence to boldly embrace God's command to love and the commission of Jesus to serve. Their communication styles changed from harsh thunder to enlightened, assertive and loving Grace.

They and the other disciples took the baton of salvation from the hand of their martyred master and as bold and extraordinary children of God, they set out with divine purpose to make a difference as the apostles of love, and ambassadors from the kingdom of heaven.

John 14:12 *"Truly, truly, I say to you, whoever believes in me will also do the works that I do; and greater works than these he will do, because I am going to the Father."*

Matthew 28:14 *"Therefore go and make disciples of all nations."*

1. God is Light (Life Application Study Bible)

The Incarnation of the Word of Life

1 John 1:1 *"That which was from the beginning, which we have heard, which we have seen with our eyes, which we have looked at and our hands have touched- this we* proclaim concerning the word of life."

2. The life appeared. We have seen it and testify to it.
3. We proclaim to you that we have seen and heard, so that you also may have fellowship with us.

In John 17:21-22 Jesus prays for all believers, *"that all of them may be one, Father, just as you are in me, and I am in you. May they also be in us so that the world may believe that you have sent me. ...so that they may be brought to complete unity."*

Love and Hatred

1 John 2:3 *"We know that we have come to know him if we keep his commands. Whoever says, 'I know him,' but does not do what he commands is a liar. But anyone who hates a brother or sister is in the darkness."*

In the book *"Love is a Decision,"* by Gary Smalley with John Trent, PhD, we are reminded that love is work. Fighting for it is the most healthy and lasting because it is a reflection of how much we honor the ones we love. God's grace gets us over the rough spots.

In "The 5 Love Languages" by Gary Chapman, Gary and the Apostle Paul Unite and we learn how to express heartfelt commitment to our spouses in discerning and speaking the love language that is particularly affirmational to them.

The authors long research and experience with couples has yielded five general ways that romantic partners express and experience love that is the secret to love that last.

1. Words of affirmation
2. Acts of service
3. Receiving Gifts
4. Quality Time
5. Physical Touch

1 Corinthians 13 is cited in this book of scripture inspired by unconditional and sacrificial love. It took the ministry and sacrifice of Jesus to teach us how to love and respect each other with patience and the merciful grace God blessed us with. We can never match the perfection of Jesus, but we can honor him in our daily strivings to be the best possible Christ-like versions of ourselves.

Reasons for Writing

1 John 2:12-14 *"I am writing to you, dear children, because your sins have been forgiven on account of his name. Because you know the Father…from the beginning. I am writing to you, fathers, because you know him who is from the beginning. I am writing to you young men because you have overcome the evil one."*

Not Loving the World

1 John 2:15-16 *"Do not love the world or anything in the world, for the lust of the flesh, the lust of the eyes, and the pride of life comes not from the Father, but from the world."*

Warnings Against Denying the Son

1 John 2:18 *"Dear children, this is the last hour, and as you have heard, that the anti-Christ is coming, even now many antichrists have come."*

There are over one hundred warnings and references to false teachers in the Holy Bible, mostly in the New Testament; I think because this is when the spirit of Jesus appears in the flesh and satan can't handle the truth! He does not want us to be free!

"John wrote about the most vital aspects of faith so that his readers would know Christian truth from error." (Life Applications Study Bible).

How many know of errors that are made intentionally are just old fashioned lies?

1 John 2:26 *"I am writing these things to you about those who are trying to lead you astray."* Misery loves company.

1 John 3:1-3 *"See what great love the Father has lavished on us, that we should be called children of God." And that is what we are! The reason the world does not know us is that it did not know him. But we know that when Christ appears, we shall be like him for we shall see him as he is."* (unity in diversity in the Body of Christ).

1 John 3:8 "The reason the Son of God appeared was to destroy the devils work."

From the Gospel of the Kingdom by George Eldon Ladd., page 55 *"Yes, the Kingdom of God is here, but instead of destroying human sovereignty, it has attacked the sovereignty of Satan…instead of making changes in the external political order of things, Jesus is making changes in the spiritual order in the lives of men and women."*

John 3:9 *"No one who is born of God will continue to sin, because God 's seed remains in them."*

Matthew 13:31-32 *"The Kingdom of Heaven is like a mustard seed. Though it is the smallest of all seeds, yet when it grows it is the largest of garden plants and becomes a tree, so that the birds come and perch in its branches."*

Question: Who are the birds? WE ARE!

More on Love and Hatred

1 John 3:11-12 *"For this is the message you have heard from the beginning: we should love one another." Do not be like Cain, who killed his own brother. Do not be surprised my brothers and sisters, if the world hates you. We know that we have passed from death to life because we love each other."* (The Greatest Commandment Saves)

On Denying the Incarnation

1 John 4:1-3 *"Dear friends, do not believe every spirit, but test the spirits to see whether they are from God. But every spirit that does not acknowledge Jesus is not from God."*

God's Love and Ours

1 John 4:8-9 *"Who ever does not love does not know God. This is how God showed his love among us; he sent his one and only son into this world that we might live through him."*

1 John 4:21 *"And he has given us this command: anyone who loves God must also love his brother and sister."*

Matthew 22:34-40 (The Greatest Commandment)

Faith in the Incarnate Son of God

1 John 5:1 *"Everyone who believes that Jesus is the Christ is born of God, and everyone who loves the father loves his child as well."*

John reminds us of the light that was *"in the beginning"* (Genesis), the word of God that was God incarnate as his *"one and only son"* on earth. (John 1:1-4)

Galatians 3:26 *"So in Christ Jesus you are all children of God through faith, baptized into Christ, clothe yourself with Christ...all one in Christ."*

Galatians 3:28 *"There is neither Jew nor Gentile, neither slave nor free, nor is there male and female for as you are alone in Christ."*

Romans 8:17 *"Now if we are children of God, then we are heirs of God and co-heirs with Christ."*

1 John 5:4 *"For anyone born of God overcomes the world. Whoever has the son has life; whoever does not have the son, does not have life."*

Concluding Affirmations

1 John 5:13 *"Know that you have eternal life. This is the confidence we have in approaching God, that if we ask anything according to his will, he hears us."*

"When we talk to God, we shouldn't demand what we want; rather, we should ask him (for) what he wants for us." (Life Application Study Bible)

If we are sanctified and baptized children of God, we pray first for others, and then for things God knows are good for us and not out of lust or greed or harmful to us or others.

1 John 5:18 "We know that anyone born of God does not continue to sin; the one who has born of God keeps them safe.

1 John 5:20 "We know also that the Son of God has come and has given us understanding."

So, what do we do with a whole bible full of spirit and understanding? Never sin again? We were wonderfully made imperfect. Under the Kingdom's salvation and sanctification, we have the freedom to obey God,(or not) and a supernatural desire and ability to check ourselves before we wreck ourselves.

1 John 5:20 *"Understanding, so that we may know him who is true. And we are in him who is true by being in his son. Jesus Christ: he is the true God and eternal life."*

The Son of Thunder may not be quite so full of vim and vinegar as an elder statesman, but he can still speak Jesus and still bring the Thunder and Lightning!

(play *"I Speak Jesus"* by, Charity Gayle, live)

The world is in a battle with generational curses of dysfunction: Mental, emotional, and physical abuse. Manipulating and exploiting children. Chaos, crime, and death for insults.

This circle must be broken. Isiah 9:2 "Those who walked in darkness have seen a radiant light shining on them. They once lived in the shadows of death but now a glorious light has dawned." Isiah is the most quoted prophet of the Bible.

CHAPTER 6

Truth and love in 2 John.

Purpose: To emphasize the basics of following Christ- truth and love.

Original Audience: The lady chosen by God and her children.

Date written: About the same time as 1 John.

Setting: Likely written to a woman and her family who were members of a church overseen by John with whom John had developed a strong relationship. John was, once again, warning of the false teachers who were becoming prevalent in some of the churches. .

Key Verse: *"And this is love: that we walk in obedience to his commands. As you have heard from the beginning, his command is that you walk in love."* (1:16)

Theme Explanation

Truth: Following God's Word, the Bible is essential to Christian living because God is the author of all truth. To be loyal to Christ's teachings, we must seek to know the Bible and must never twist its message to our own needs or purposes or encourage others who misuse it. Christ's true followers consistently obey this truth.

Love: Christ's command is for Christians to love one another. This is the basic ingredient of True Christianity. To obey Christ fully, we must follow His command to love others. Helping, giving and meeting the needs are ways that we put love into practice.

False Teachers: We must be wary of religious leaders who are not true to Christ's teachings, and we must not give them a platform to spread false teaching. Don't encourage those who are opposed to Christ. Politely remove yourself from association with false teachers. Be aware of what is being taught in your church. (Life Application Study Bible)

1 Watch out for false teachers (Life Application Study Bible)

2 John 1: *"The elder,*

To the lady chosen by God and her children, whom I love in the truth, and not I only, but also all who know the truth."

2 John 2 *"Because of the truth, which lives in us and will be with us forever."*

2 John 3 *"Grace, mercy and peace from God the Father and from Jesus Christ, the Father's son, will be with us in truth and love."*

2 John 4 *"It has given me great joy to find some of your children walking in the truth, just as the Father commands us."*

2 John 5 *"I am not writing you a new command but the one we have had from the beginning. I ask that we love one another."*

2 John 6 *"And this is love; that we walk in obedience to his commands. As you have heard from the beginning, his command is that you walk in love."* (The Great Commandment is a burden only to the false teachers).

2 John 7 "I say this because many deceivers, who do not acknowledge Jesus Christ as coming in the flesh, have gone out into the world. Any such person is the deceiver and the antichrist.

2 John 8 "Watch out that you do not lose what we have worked for, but that you may be rewarded fully."

2 John 9 *"Anyone who runs ahead and does not continue in the teaching of Christ does not have God; whoever continues in the teaching has both the Father and the Son."*

The truth is that we love Jesus, not only that he suffered and died for us that we might have a new life of peace and hope, but because in the following of him, we see the great contrast between a fallen world of self-serving merchants of deceptive practices and Jesus who is truth and love personified. Real love is selfless and giving, empathetic and compassionate without conditions. Real love is not clever or sly.

(play *"I'll Fly Away"* by, Alison Krauss and Gillian Welch, lyrics)

CHAPTER 7

Encouragement, joy, and hospitality 3rd John

Purpose: To commend Gaius for his hospitality and encourage him in his Christian life.

Original Audience: Gaius, a prominent Christian in one of the churches known to John.

Date Written: Same estimated time span as John's previous two epistles.

Setting: Church leaders traveled from town to town helping establish new congregations. They depended on the hospitality of fellow believers of which Gaius was one.

Key Verse: "Dear friend, you are faithful in what you are doing for the brothers and sisters, even though they are strangers to you." (1-5)

There are no strangers in the Body of Christ. First time church attendees are considered welcomed, and valued guests. They are deliberately acknowledged and invited to a "meet and greet" with pastoral staff after each service.

John wrote to encourage those who were kind to others. Genuine hospitality was needed then and is still today. (Hospitality is a foundational element in genuine Christianity). Faithful Christian teachers and missionaries need our support, (and a sense of a United Family), extending hospitality (and support) to others will make you a partner in their ministry." (Life Application Study Bible).

1 God's children live by the standards of the Gospel. (Life Application Study Bible)

3 John 1 *"The elder, to my dear friend Gaius, whom I love in the truth."*

3 John 2 *"Dear friend, I pray that you may enjoy good health and that all may go well with you, even as your soul is getting along well."*

3 John 3 *"It gave me great joy when some believers came and testified about your faithfulness to the truth, telling how you continue to walk in it."*

3 John 5 *"Dear friend, you are faithful in what you are doing for the brothers and sisters, even though they are strangers to you. They have told the church about your love. Please send them on their way in a manner that honors God."*

3 John 9 *"I wrote to the church but Diotrephes, who loves to be first, will not welcome us."*

John adds that this man, in contrast to the servant heart of Gaius, is *"spreading malicious nonsense"* and *"even refuses to welcome other believers. He also stops those who want to (be hospitable) and puts them out of the church."*

3 John 11 *"Dear friend, do not imitate what is evil, but what is good."*

This is the eternal friction within our inner souls and in the community of fallible or malicious human beings. And it is the evidence of God's Grace: Saint John does not step out of his lane to condemn Diotrephes.

Romans 12:17-21 *"Do not repay evil for evil. Do not take revenge, my dear friends, but leave room for God's wrath, for it is written, 'It is mine to avenge; I will repay, says the Lord.' On the contrary, if your enemy is hungry; feed him, if he is thirsty; give him something to drink. In doing so, you will heap burning coals on his head.*

"For It has been said "kill 'em with kindness."

John simply and directly asserted his disappointment with Diotrephes and gracefully gave us a contrasting example.

3 John 1:12 *"Demetrius is well spoken of by everyone, and even by truth itself. We also speak well of him, and you know that tour testimony is true."*

Do we notice that, as the ancient believers and we contemporary Christians get closer to the Book of Revelation, we see a growing concern in the epistles about false teachings and false prophets who cause believers to give up on salvation and fall away from Jesus and the standard of the gospel of truth? I pray for all Christian believers and seekers of truth and the Kingdom of God on earth as it is in Heaven to remain steadfast in discernment and rebuking of the false teachers and disciples of satan, whose deliberate lust is to steal our joy.

3 John 11 "Dear friends, do not imitate what is evil but what is good. Anyone who does what is good is from God. Anyone who does what is evil has not seen God."

If we consider the Gospel standards, and examine the contrast between, these three men. We might pause and examine our own lives. Are we moving beyond the message of the Gospel and into Life Application?

Or we can just apply this simple illumination: **What Would Jesus Do? (WWJD!)**

> (play *"Somebody to You"*by, Rachael Lampa, featuring Andrew Ripp, with lyrics, 2023, clear lyrics)

CHAPTER 8

The Sin and Doom of Ungodly People and a Call to Persevere in the Book of Jude

Purpose: To remind the church of the need for constant vigilance, to keep strong the faith and the oppose heresy. *(Hersey-Opinion that is profoundly at odds with what is generally accepted)*

Author: Jude, brother of Jesus and James

Original Audience: Jewish Christians, written around AD 65

Setting: From the first century on the church has been threatened by heresy and false teaching.

Key Verse: *"Dear friends, although I was very eager to write to you about the salvation we share, I felt compelled to write you and urge you to contend for the faith that was once for all entrusted to God's holy people."* (1:3)

Jude was compelled to speak out about the dangers of false teachers and bound by a sense of duty to fight for God's truth. (1:17-25)

So, help us Father God to remember, appreciate and participate each day in the on-going process of standing firm in your word, your wisdom, your spirit and your love, the ongoing process of living in the lesson and the truth of Jesus Christ our savior, our teacher and guiding light. Amen.

1 The danger of false teachers (Life Application Study Bible)

Jude 1:1-2 Jude, a servant of Jesus Christ and a brother of James *"to those who have been called, who are loved in God the father and kept for Jesus Christ. Mercy, peace, and love be yours in obedience."*

Sin and Doom of Ungodly

Jude 4 *"For certain individuals whose condemnation was written about long ago have secretly slipped among you. They are ungodly people who pervert the grace of our God into a license from immorality and deny Jesus Christ our only sovereign Lord."*

In verse 5 Brother Jude reminds us of the hills and valleys that are the cycle of life and spiritual death, that began in the Garden of Eden with Eve's first bite of Stan's apple: The Fall.

Genesis 3:11 *"Now the serpent was more crafty than any of the wild animals the Lord God had made."*

Jude 5 *"Though you already know this, I want to remind you that the Lord at one time delivered his people out of Egypt, but later destroyed those who did not believe."*

Do any of us know of anyone whose life has been a straight line of blessings and smooth sailing, or who has been without conflict or not set back by misfortune or self-sabotage?

Jude 14-15 *"Enoch, the seventh son of Adam, prophesied about them. 'See, the Lord is coming with thousands upon thousands of his holy ones to judge everyone, and to convict all of them of all ungodly acts they have committed in their ungodliness and all the defiant words ungodly sinners have spoken against him.'"*

From "Moments of Joy" by Julie Hasling: 44 Enoch Who? "Enoch means 'dedicated' and by all means he was dedicated to God. He consistently walked with God. Enoch began walking with God at the age of 65 and continued for another 300 years until God took him to Heaven.

" ... the man didn't start walking with God until the age of 65." (I did not become a dedicated follower until age 63.) "This means there's hope for the rest of us!" (I don't know about living 300 years)

A Call to Persevere

Jude 17-23 *"But dear friends, remember what the Apostles of our Lord Jesus Christ foretold. They said to you in the last times there will be scoffers who will follow their own ungodly desires. These are the people who divide you, who follow mere natural instincts and do not have the spirit. But you, dear friends, by building yourselves up in your most holy faith, and praying in the holy spirit., keep yourselves in God's love as you wait for the mercy of our Lord Jesus Christ to bring you eternal life. Be merciful to those who doubt. Save others by snatching them from the fire; to others show mercy, mixed with fear, hating even the clothing stained by corrupted flesh."*

(play *"Scars"* by, I am They, lyrics)

CHAPTER 9

The Revelation from Jesus

Purpose: To reveal the full identity of Jesus Christ and to give warning and hope to believers

Author: The apostle John

Original Audience: The seven churches in Asia and all believers everywhere

Date Written: Approximately AD95

Where Written: On the Island of Patmos

Setting: Most interpreters believe the seven churches of Asia to whom John wrote were experiencing persecutions under Emperor Titus Flavius Domitian (AD 90-95).

The Roman authorities had exiled the venerable apostle to the Island of Patmos because he would have been more dangerous to them as another martyr and eyewitness to Jesus Christ. In his isolation, John had a vison of the glorified Christ. God also revealed to John what would take place in the future, the coming judgment, and the ultimate triumph of God over evil.

Key Verse: *"Blessed is the one who reads aloud the words of this prophecy, and blessed are those who hear it and take to heart what is written in it, because the time is near."* (1:3)

Special Features: Revelation is apocalyptic -a type of Jewish literature that uses, symbolic imagery to communicate hope in the ultimate triumph of God to those suffering from persecution. Events are ordered according to literary rather than strictly chronological patterns. (Life Application Study Bible)

Revelation is a book of hope. John: beloved Apostle and eyewitness of Jesus, proclaimed that the victorious Lord would surely return to vindicate the righteous and judge the wicked. But Revelation is also a book of warning. Things were not as they should have been in the first century churches, so through John, Jesus called the members to commit themselves *to "live in righteousness."* (Life Application Study Bible)

Prologue

Revelation 1-5 *"The revelation from Jesus Christ, which God gave him was to show his servants what must soon take place. He made it known by sending his angels to his servant John, who testifies to everything he saw, that is, the word of God and the testimony of Jesus Christ. Blessed is the one who reads aloud the words of this prophecy, and blessed are those who hear it and take to heart what is written in it, because the time is near. To the seven churches in the province of Asia; grace and peace to you and from him who is and who was, and who is to come and from the seven spirits before his throne, and from Jesus Christ, who is the faithful witness, the first born of the dead, the first resurrected and the ruler of the kings of the earth."*

John is reminding us that God loves us enough to set us free from our sin nature by his Grace and Jesus' Sacrifice. He wants us to know that we belong to the Kingdom of the High Priest of Service; to God and his children in need, and that in this service is eternal glory and power.

Revelation 7-8 *"Look, he is coming in the clouds, and every eye will see him, even those who precede him. 'I am the Alpha and the Omega, says the Lord God, who is, and who was, and who is to come, the Almighty.'"*

(play *"Jesus is Coming Back"* by, Jordan Feliz, featuring Johnathan Taylor)

John's Vision of Christ

Revelation 1:10 *"'On the Lord's Day, said John, 'I was in the spirit, and I heard behind me a loud voice like a trumpet, which said, write on a scroll what you see and send it to the seven churches; to Ephesus, Smyrna, Pergamum, Thyatira, Sardis, Philadelphia, and Laodicea.'"*

Revelation 1:17-20 "When I saw him, I fell at his feet as though dead. Then he placed his right hand on me and said, 'do not be afraid, I am the first and the last. I am the living one; I was dead, and now look, I am alive forever and ever! And I hold the keys of death and Hades.

19 Write therefore what you have seen, what is now and what will take place later. 20 The mystery of the seven stars that you saw in my righthand and of the seven golden lamp stands is this; the seven stars are the angels of the seven churches, and the seven lampstands are the seven churches.'"

Jesus holds the keys of death and Hades (hell). He alone can free us from eternal bondage to satan. He alone has the power and authority to set us free from Sins control… *"Believers don't have to fear Hades or death. Instead, we must turn from sin and turn to Jesus in faith."* (Life Application Study Bible).

In Revelation 2, John's opening remarks to each church, the Lord of the universe, who was guiding him, knew their circumstances and particular persecutions for the practice of their faith in Jesus as divine. John praised and encouraged them for their perseverance in afflictions, deeds of love, tolerance, being holy and as true and faithful witnesses to God's creation. Then came the admonishments and guidance to correct their failures.

Hills and valleys. Grace and mercy. Creation, The Fall, Redemption and Resurrection. God loves us too much to leave us where we are. Jesus loves every Church and everybody in the Body of Christ.

(play *"Hills and Valleys"* by, Taurin Wells)

Jesus wants each of us to be the best possible versions of ourselves, under God. This means in accordance with his word and spirit.

Our Pastor David brought an encouraging and uplifting message on Revelation in June 2023. It was about the Nation of Israels cycle of decline and rebirth: Hills and valleys. Creation, a falling back, redemption and restoration. (*sounds like my life*). If you have been around long enough, you can relate. Life is a cycle. The apostle Paul preaches joy in all circumstances. That is how he managed to live life to the full.

Pastor David cited the latest re-birth of the Nation of Israel in 1948, compliments of the United Nations after the devastation of Europe and genocide of the European Jews during WWII. He said *"Don't be anxious or angry. Be intentional (in love, faith, etc.), we are in a spiritual battle (the spirit of chaos is the enemy). Don't rebuke fools (misguided) being used by satan. God has a plan-Revelation. People will be judged or redeemed."*

So, we CAN hold on to our faith, our wits, and our walk with Jesus in our servant hearts.

Pastor David *"God says love your enemy. Rise above the chaos and division. Maintain unity and diversity in the body of Christ. Be intentional for Jesus. Our neighbors are not the enemy. satan is the common enemy. He is destined to fail and fall into the fiery lake of sulfur."*

Heavenly Warrior Defeats the Battle

Revelation 19:12-13 *"His eyes are like blazing fire, and on his head are many crowns. He has a name written on him that no one knows but himself. He is dressed in a robe dipped in blood, and his name is the word of God."*

"The Book of Revelation Made Easy," by Kenneth L. Gentry, Jr. TH. D. "Revelation explains, justifies, and warns about the removal of Jerusalem from Israel. Earlier, during Jesus 'earthly ministry, Israel is prepared for the change."

Matthew 8:11-12 *"But the sons of the Kingdom shall be cast out into the outer darkness, in that place there will be weeping and gnashing of teeth."*

John's visions were graphic; full of symbolism, both disturbing and hopeful, and consistent with the Old Testament prophecies regarding the destruction of Israel (notably the Roman decimation of the

Temple in Jerusalem). His visions also included the second coming of Jesus in the cloud along with Redemption and Restoration in the New Heaven and the earth.

Gentry "Though the grand images in Revelation are not literal, they do portray historical events."

The temple of Jerusalem was utterly destroyed, and Israel's survivors were dramatically scattered in AD70.

Gentry "From Revelation 21:1 through 22:5, John describes this New Creation Bride (that symbolically replaces the symbolic Harlet of blasphemy in Revelation 17) and paints an ideal picture of the Christian faith in time and on earth. John paints a glorious picture of the redemption effected by Christ: It Initiates in seed principle the New Creation, which ultimately results in the consummate, fall and perfect eternal order."

A New Heaven and a New Earth

Revelation 12;1 "I saw a new Heaven and a new earth, for the First Heaven and the first earth had passed away, and there was no longer any sea. I saw the Holy City the new Jerusalem, coming down out of heaven from God, prepared by as a bride beautifully dressed for her husband. And I heard a loud voice from the throne saying, "Look! God's dwelling place is now among the people, and he will dwell with them. They will be his people, and God himself, will be with them and be their God. He will wipe away every tear from their eyes. There will be no more death, or mourning, or crying or pain, for the old order of things has passed away. He who was seated on the throne said, "I am making everything new.! Then he said, "Write this down, for these words are trustworthy and true."

Jeremiah 31:31-34 "The days are coming, declares the Lord, when I will make a new covenant with the people of Israel and with the people of Judah. It will not be like the covenant I made with their ancestors when I took them by the hand and led them out of Egypt, because they broke my covenant, though I was a husband to them, declares the Lord. This is the covenant I will make with the people of Israel after that time, declares the Lord.

I will put my law in their minds, and I will all write it on their hearts. I will be their God, and they will be my people. No longer will they teach their neighbor, or say to one another, 'Know the Lord', because they will all know me, from the least of them to the greatest, declares the Lord. For I will forgive their wickedness and will remember their sins no more."

And I think that the vaccinations of chaos in the valleys give us a healing gratitude above complacency in the hills of vision, peace; and as the Apostle Paul prescribes, Joy in All Circumstances-knowing Jesus and your servant hearts. Thank You Jesus, to whom I say Yes and AMEN!

(play *"Yes and Amen"* by, Chris Tomlin, lyrics/video)

Consistency, Detail, Socratic Teaching, Epistemology, and Apologetics

I believe in God the Father, Jesus Christ our Savior and Teacher, the Holy Spirit: our helper, comforter, intercessor, our advocate before God, our judge and the Holy Spirt of truth that sets us free.

The word of our Bible is detailed and consistent beyond human limits, manifesting ultimate goodness over evil and my selfish thoughts and ways. And the truth in the Gospel can also be seen in how much evil hates and fears God's word, wisdom, spirit and love.

The teachings of Jesus are Socratic: Not dogmatic but eliciting though and contentment versus planting thoughts sown with shame, doubt, deceit, vindictive and intolerance.

God's word stands upright in the test of time and epistemology, which is the investigation of what distinguishes justified belief from mere opinion. *(Sometimes "Wind and fury; signifying nothing")*.

The life and lesson of Jesus Christ stands upright in Apologetics; from the Greek word Apologia- A reasoned defense.

The Kingdom of God came to the world in human form two thousand years ago and mankind could have rejected it. Instead, we now, and from this day forward, rise to reject satan and his minions by walking with Jesus.

God designed humans in his image (according to Psalm 8), just a little lower than angels. With free will, we are tested, and we don't take goodness for granted.

We were purposely designed to be creatures with free will so we would understand the difference between right and wrong, good / and evil, and so to appreciate goodness and the righteous choices we will make more consistently.

God made us (each of his children), with the potential of Jesus. Not to stress over imperfections and so give up the Holy Ghost, but under God, to thrive in union with our Savior and Redeemer.

(play *"Sunday Morning Feeling"* by, Apollo LTD featuring Ryan Stevenson, official lyric video)

CHAPTER 10

Battle Plan / Inner Disciple

(Part A) Get in the Kitchen

1) Publish and distribute book: TRANSFRORMATION (stone font on the cover.) Coming to Know Jesus and your Servant Heart. (hard cover version)

2) Use unrestricted Edwardian Script ITC font family for Emphasis as warranted.

3) Create coat tail products written in Edwardian Script ITC family font for Psalms, Proverbs, Parables, Prayers, Poems, etc.

4) Create a TRANSFORMATION social media page and web site for the General Public and one for reader and author fellowship.

5) Hire a fiduciary, create an LLC, and make a last will and testimony.

6) Contract with a local printing company to produce and deliver coat tail written products. (Proceeds, from any product including

the original and copywritten cloud cross image over a field, to be rendered to the photo owner Angela Stout; marketing designation- Angel a for Jesus)

7) Market coat tail products under Servant King Productions / God Wink Media, LLC. .

8) Pay off personal debt and hire a publicist with initial proceeds from the TRANSFORMATION book and coat tail products sales.

9) Bring to a boil, stir, simmer, cook and serve until each marketing trend cools.

(Part B) Outreach

1) Reach out to K-Love parent company and publishing entity — Educational Media Foundation (EMF) 800-323- 9473 www.emfmedia.com to propose AUDIO BOOK version of TRANSFORMATION book with Christian music video suggestions from the TRANSFORMATION book. Publish, Produce, and distribute under Servant King Productions/God Wink Media LLC .... Cook, stir, serve.

(Part C) Praise and Worship Ministry

Reach out to K-Love Radio to propose an American and Global Perpetual Ministry of Christian Music Concerts with Encouraging and Joyous Song, Evangelism, Teaching, and Testimonies. The Ministry creation will consist of a Large Team of Christian bands and solo artists divided into Squads rotating on and off the Battlefield to keep the Christians fresh and satan gasping.

1) Each Squad will consist of a FELLOWSHIP of Artists, Promotors, Producers, Pastors, Directors, Roadies, Support Staff, etc.

2) Partner with Dallas Jenkins and Angel Studios with producers and actors from "The Chosen" appearing in the Praise and Worship Ministry rotation to compliment, nurture and preserve the Fellowship of each Squad. The Transformation and Angel cohorts will commune, encourage, and energize each other.

3) Testimonials can be from Preachers, Teachers, Theologians, Musicians and the rich and famous but mostly from ordinary, average people who were Brave enough to conquer their demons and Bold enough to shout out the Joy of Salvation, Purpose, and New Life!... Bold, Average, Beautiful Believers. PARRHESIA IDIOTAS!

4) Community Revival Service Ministries will occur in conjunction with and in proximity to the concert events. This Ministry will be financed by an Evangelical Philanthropical Charitable 501©3 nonprofit, seed funded by a 51% dedication of funds from proceeds of TRANSFORMATION books and the coat tail products. (The first 10% to my church, Our Savior's Church of Louisiana)

5) Solicitation of corporate sponsorships will augment the funding, bringing prestige and public good will to the participating corporations whose logos will appear in promotions, advertisements and adorn the concert sets.

6) Established nonprofit community organizing agencies, local churches and government agencies will assist with logistics, manpower and volunteer recruitment. Examples may include (but not be limited to) The Robert L. Woodson Center

(woodsoncenter.org) for community empowering, revitalization and crime reduction; the WMCA, Boys and Girls Clubs, Interfaith Ministries, the Salvation Army and The Adult and Teen Challenge for addictions.

7) Additional funding and human capital will come from local community organizations, churches, private citizens, and local business donations. Federal grants like SAMHSA for mental health and addictions may contribute.

(Part D) Chronological WRITTEN iterations of the TRANSFORMATION Book

1) Coffee Table version of TRANSFORMATION book with scripture relevant art works, from ancient to modern times. Eg. From Michelangelo to Akiane Kramarik. Cook, stir, serve.

2) Commission an author to Create a book on the Foundational and Providential Nature of the US Constitution with Biblical contextual reference and REVERANCE. Produce, Publish and Distribute. Cook, stir, serve.

3) Commission an author to create a Children's version of TRANSFORMATION for tandem release with the Constitution book. .... Cook, stir, serve.

4) Produce and distribute paperback version of TRANSFORMATION. Cook, stir, serve.

Stan Rynott, MA, LSCW, C o G
Stan d for Jesus 03/7/ 2024

Battle plan subject to evolution and modification relevant to changing circumstances and ancillary input.

How we come to know our Inner Disciple

John 13:35 "By this everyone will know that you are my disciples; if you love one another."

Pastor Scott "A Disciple is someone who Follows, learns from and Imitates Jesus."

We lead first by example and then in The Word.

Colossians 1:9-10 "For this reason, since we heard about you, we have not stopped praying for you. We continually ask God to fill you with the knowledge of his will through all the wisdom and understanding that the Spirit gives, so that you may live a life worthy of the Lord and please him in every way: bearing fruit in every good work."

Pastor Scott "Success is not what you persue; it's who you attract by the person you become."

When we receive Grace from God, we are super naturally inclined to pay it forward.

When we care enough about people to be gracious and patient knowing none of us knows the other's circumstances.

CLOSING ARGUMENTS

In the beginning there was light, and that light still has not been extinguished.

The apostle Paul was certainly not a counselor to Jesus Christ, but he was like and advocate attorney counselor; just as Moses, Abraham, Isaac, and Jacob before him; and so also among his peers: John, James, Peter, Matthew, Mark and Luke and the rest. They all serve as a voice for God and Divine Ambassadors. Saints for and in the Kingdom of Heaven.

Like skilled attorneys, they presented the case for the Gospel of Jesus, clearly and forthrightly; under God the Father, inspired by Jesus and led by the Holy Spirit of truth.

What would Paul say in Jesus 'name? He would make a clear case for deliberate Christianity. *"And finally, brothers and sisters, rejoice! Strive for a full restoration. Encourage one another. Be of one mind. Live in peace. And the God of love and peace will be with you."*

Apologetics

Apologetics is From the Greek apologia, which means "speaking in defense." It is the discipline of defending religious doctrines through systematic argumentation and civil discourse.

In books like "Evidence for Jesus" and "Evidence that Demands a Verdict," by Josh and Sean McDowell; the authors are often former agnostics or atheists, who in angry attempts in research to convict Christianity of fraud were instead convicted, themselves as deliberate Christians and faithful followers Jesus.

C. S. Lewis, who is cited in this book, was formerly an angry atheist who was saved and soldiered on to write "Mere Christianity," "The Most Reluctant Convert", "The Chronicles of Narnia" series, and many more.

I, Stanley Rynott, only discovered that I was blessed by my Lord, Savior, Teacher and Guiding Light, Jesus Christ of Heaven, and Nazareth in March of 2017. I was a 63-year-old toddler Christian. Deliberately, now I hope to bring the overcoming love of God's encouragement for others to recognize the blessings of Jesus and Your Potential in the Kingdom; on earth as it is in Heaven.

Hills and valleys are the bumps and pit- falls on the crossroads of life: From Adam and Eve to Cain and Abel; from the dark Tower of Babel to the Light and Truth of Jesus we find in our Faith: Encouragement and Confidence to persevere in gratitude for all the scars of victory along the road to the Kingdom of Heaven; with Jesus at our side, the Holy Spirit inside and the Holy Father going out before us.

What are you willing to do to grow in your faith, find direction and peace and increase the Kingdom? Will you immerse yourself in the body of Christ more regularly and in person rather than streaming Sunday service from your living room?

Will you bring the Holy Spirit fellowship of the sanctuary through the doors of the Church of Jesus Christ and down the street to the grocery store, the restaurant, the hardware store and greet the people you contact there as a connection with a CoG-Child of God and not just a cog in a machine? Will you call them by the name on their tag and lift them up in the spirit you found in church and small group fellowship?

Will you consider the blessing of joining a small group and hearing the word and receiving the spirit as a booster shot to the weekly church experience?

There is statistical evidence that people who pray and or engage in Christian fellowship at least three or four times a week are measurably happier than those who merely attend church on Sunday.

(Play "Sunday Sermons" by Ann Wilson)

The Pastor of the church I attend has, in recent years, renamed the small group Bible studies as Discipleship Groups which seems like an obvious move based on the Greatest Commandment from God to love others; and the blessing of the Opportunity of the Great Commission to be a part of something bigger than ourselves.

The Power of Fellowship / Brotherhood

The American Heritage dictionary defines Brotherhood: An association of men or women, united for a common purpose and fraternity or union in Fellowship - the companionship of individuals in a congenial atmosphere and on equal terms. (Under God we thrive in diversity.)

God made us on purpose for purpose. We are less prisoners of the flesh if we are in His Purpose. God did not create us to be alone. He created us to be one of many in a fellowship of purpose with a spirit of harmony. Just as Jesus said to the Father "...that all of them may be one, Father, just as you are in me, and I am in you."

Consider the motto of a rag tag group that would rise to what would become the greatest country on the face of the earth. The 13 British colonies were re-named and re- born as America the Beautiful. And that "One Nation Under God" went out with God and defeated the globe's greatest army and tool of the tyrants of those times.

The thirteen colonies, collectively, were like a mighty David that slew Goliath. And then they had the audacity to create a God blessed Constitution of liberty and justice for all… E pluribus Unum! - Out of many one! And, yes there was trial, error and growth on that long and winding road. There is a mix of good and bad in all individuals and groups. Only Jesus, newborn babies and God's Kingdom are blameless.

In 1776 founding fathers were engaged in a battle for righteousness in a cause, that if lost, would result in their collective hangings as traitors to the tyrants of England. The tyrants lost, the world shook and the oppressed took heart.

Romans 6: Slaves to Righteousness

6:17 *"But thanks be to God that, though you used to be slaves to sin, you have come to obey from your heart the pattern of teaching that now has claimed your allegiance. 18 You have been set free from sin and have become slaves to righteousness."*

Emmett Fox. *"Can human nature change? Shallow thinkers sometimes say doggedly and pessimistically that 'You can't change human nature.'"*

But under God, all things are possible! It took the entire course of our lives to arrive at the habits, routines, attitudes, communication styles, behaviors and addictions that define our presence and plight here on earth.

It will take discernment, desire, motivation, the power of daily prayer and devotion to Jesus, our higher power to overcome the past and realize God's purpose and our Servant Hearts.

(play *"Take me Back"* by, Cochren & Co., lyric video)

Romans 8: Life Through the Spirit

Romans 8:28 *"And we know that in all things God works for the good of those who love him, who have been called according to his purpose."*

My Testimony

By the time I was invited to Our Savior's Church in March of 2017, I had not been a regular church attendee since I left my family in 1975. In that long lost season, I quit my family, church, and college to get a job and get married to my future ex-wife. (Patience is a virtue, a blessing and one of the Fruits of the Spirit in Galatians 5:22-23.)

Fast forward to 2017: Immersed in the worship music, the Holy Spirit power of the sanctuary and the moto of our church: to "Know God, Find Freedom, Discover Purpose and Make a Difference", I experienced an awakening of Affirmation, Inspiration and Aspiration.

I was re-Affirmed and ignited as a Deliberate Christian and Inspired by a cause greater than myself with an Aspiration to make contributions to my church, my family, and communities. And at this writing, to all my readers and anyone who cares to hear the word of God and contemplate the Life and Lesson of Jesus Christ, our Savior, Teacher and inextinguishable and inspirational Guiding Light; You ARE a New Creation. By the Truth of Jesus we are free.

>   Play *("Truth be Told"* by, Matthew West, official music video)

And now to fulfill the promise and challenge I made to you early on and among these pages. I am leaving a dozen lined pages to write "Your Testimony." No worries, no hurry.

I wrote most of this book by my own hand because I am a cognitive klutz with information technology and a digital (fingers) klutz on the keyboard.

>   Today is September 17, the Year of Our Lord 2023.

In writing this book, I used up many pages of scratch paper and countless 6 packs of correction tape. Yes, Father God, you are my Heavenly Father, Jesus Christ is my Savior, Teacher, and Guiding Light. The Holy Spirit is my Comforter, Helper, my Advocate before you and my Holy Spirit of Truth.

And yes, Brothers and Sisters, in the Kingdom of Heaven on earth, all things are possible and human nature Will Change. Life is scratch paper and under God, correction tape is not rejection!

We need not fret over governments, the politics of division and destruction or chaos let loose in the streets. Jesus did not come to overturn administrations. He is here to rebuke satan, but not to change the political order of disorder. Jesus walked among us in the flesh 2023 years ago and in the spirit today to change the spiritual order of men and women. Jesus died for our salvation and, for some, to take up his mission to change the world for the better.

We ARE better together. Unity in diversity is overcoming prejudice and censorship with the power of love and a default position of patience and Grace from God. Amazing Grace. We pay it forward.

If we deliberately dwell in the Body of Christ, breathe in the Peace of the Holy Spirit Breeze and Blossom in the Bosom of Fellowship, we will Know Jesus, break the chains of fear, discrimination and addictions; Discover Purpose, make a Difference and Overcome the World; one soul at a time.

Your Testimony

Take your time and let your writings be the method of the clarification of your thoughts and the perfection of your story telling. (Scratch paper). And by prayer and petition, may peace be with you in the wonderful execution of your ongoing journey coming to know Jesus and your Servant Heart.

(Play You Will be Found by Natalie Grant, featuring Corey Asbury)

(Space provided after Play List)

(play *The Blessing,* by Kari Jobe and Cody Carnes, live from Elevation Ballantyne/ Elevation Worship)

"Your testimony makes you a part of this book in the Community and Fellowship of Deliberate Christians. The most important attribute of Christianity, other than Christ, is Relationships. We ARE Better Together!"

As I was growing up in the late 60's and early 70's, Church and Christian music is not what moved me. The music my friends and I absorbed from the radio waves spoke to troubles, truth and beauty. The lyrics and the melodies seemed to be written specifically for each individual and their circumstances. Those songs were and are the chorus of our lives. They connect us and we were all shaped and motivated by the musical and cultural zeitgeist of our developmental years.

I started listening to K - Love radio in the summer of 2017 and found myself awakening to a deeper spiritual level of awareness of what is possible walking with Jesus. Lately, I have become enamored with finding God in the popular secular music of my youth and today. Positive and Encouraging music is a Gift from God. Music shows us that we have much more in common than the things that try to separate us in this chaotic politically charged, cancel culture society. Worship music shook my world and catalyzed my New Life in Christ at Our Saviors Church in my March Spring in the year of Our Lord 2017.

(play My Sweet Lord by George Harrison)

You are all Partners of the Prize

The goal is Expand the Kingdom of Heaven, ReStore and Increase Regular Church Attendance, Promote Small Group Bible Study Fellowship and Animate The Descendants of "The Maker's Dozen."

LOOK FOR THE ONLINE FORUM WHERE YOU AND OTHER READERS CAN COMMUNE WITH EACH OTHER AND THE AUTHOR

Look for "stand for Jesus."

"My Testimony"

"Name:_____   Date:"_____

_____

_____

_____

_____

_____

_____

_____

_____

_____

_____

_____

TRANSFORMATION PLAY LIST

Love God love people by Danny Gokey
God so loved the world by we the Kingdom.
Peace on earth by Austin French
Nobody by Casting Crowns with Matthew West
Joy in the morning by Tauren Wells
Tell your heart to breathe again by Danny Gokey
Same God by Elevation Worship
Joy to the world traditional
living hope by Phil Wickham
If I can dream. Elvis Presley hologram with Céline Dion
Amazing Grace by Phil Wickham
Amazing Grace (my chains are broken) Chris Tomlin
Gratitude by Brandon Lake
Joyful by Dante Bowe
Onward Christian soldiers, traditional
Child of love by we the Kingdom
For the good by Riley Clemmons
Thank God I do by Lauren Daigle
Then Christ came by Phil Wickham
What the World Needs Now is Love by Dionne Warwick
Way maker by Michael W. Smith
Marry did you know by Pentatonix.
Name of Jesus by Chris Tomlin
How Far by Tasha Layton

Brighter days by Blessing Offor
Let love win by Andrew Ripp
Don't lose heart by Stephen Curtis Chapman
Perfectly by loved by Rachel Lampa and Toby Mac
Born again by Austin French
The River by Jordan Feliz
Running Home by Cochren and Company
Jesus changed my life by Katie Nicole
In Jesus name by Katie Nicole
For the love of God by Andrew Ripp
Chain breaker by Zach Williams
Rescue by Lauren Daigle
His eye is on the Sparrow by Gladys Knight
Overcomer by Mandisa R I P
God so loved the world by We the Kingdom
Burn the ships by For King and Country
Joy in the morning by Tauren Wells
That's Enough by Brandon Heath
My Jesus by Anne Wilson
Heaven in the New World by Steven Curtis Chapman
Redeemed by Big Daddy Weave
Cornerstone by Toby Mack
Amazing Grace by Rosemary Siemans
Less like me by Zach Williams
Haven't seen it yet by Danny Gokey
Believe for it by Ce Ce Winans
Carry on wayward son by Kansas.
Alive and Breathing by Matt Maher
What are we waiting for? By For King and Country
The Great Adventure by Steven Curtis Chapman
Good morning, Mercy by Jason Crabb
The Goodness by Toby Mac with Blessing Offor
Swingin' by Thad Cockrell
When the Saints go Marching in

I Can Only Imagine by Mercy Me
The Lord's Prayer by Matt Maher
Give Me Your Eyes By Brandon Heath
That's Enough by Brandon Heath
You say by Lauren Daigle
Good God Almighty by Crowder
One Thing Remains (your love never fails) by Jesus Culture
Healing by Blanca
Oxygen by Lincoln Brewster
Too Good to Not Believe by Brandon Lake
Running home by Cochran and company
Say I won't by Mercy Me
Revolutionary by Josh Wilson
He Ain't Heavy, He's My Brother, by The Hollies
The Goodness by Blessing Offor and Toby Mac
Cornerstone by TobyMac with Zach Williams
The Lord's Prayer by Matt Maher
Relate by For King and Country
The Goodness of God by Ce Winans
Let it Be by The Beatles
Nothing Else by Cody Carnes
There Was Jesus by Zach Williams with Dolly Parton
Rockin' Pneumonia and the Boogie Woogie Flu by Johny Rivers
Fingerprints by Dan Bremnes
I Can Only Imagine by Mercy Me
Hold On by Katy Nichole
Christ in me by Jeremy Camp
Material World by Madonna
Love God Love People by Danny Gokey
The King is Alive by Jordan Feliz
This Little Light of Mine. Listener Kids on You Tube
Soul on Fire by Third Day
For the good by Riley Clemens
Desert Road by Casting Crowns

I' am so Blessed by Cain
Child of God by Crowder
Fear No More by Building 49
See Me Through it by Brandon Heath
People are Crazy by Billy Currington
First Things First by Consumed by Fire
Fear is Not my Future by Maverick City Music
I Speak Jesus by Charity Gayle
I'll Fly Away by Allison Krous
Somebody to You by Rachael Lampa Featuring Andrew Ripp
Scars by I Am They
Jesus is Coming Back by Jordan Feliz and Johnathan Taylor
Hills and Valleys by Tauren Wells
Yes, and Amen by Chris Tomlin
Sunday Morning Feeling by Apollo LTD (Featuring Ryan Stevenson)
Sunday Sermons by Ann Wilson
Church (Take Me Back) by Cochren & Company
Truth Be Told by Matthew West
You Will be Found by Natalie Grant, Featuring Corey Asbury
The Blessing with Kari Jobe and Cody Carnes
My Sweet Lord by George Harrison

BIBLIOGRAPHY

The Holy Bible by God: For this book there is no substitute in anything written by the hand of man. The breath of God is the BIBLE, the Gospel- "Good news"! The possibility of New Life. The rock of the universe; eternal and boundless.

The purpose of God's word is to reveal himself to humanity. To help us to know who we really are. For better or for worse. And to give us Basic Instructions Before Leaving Earth.

May God bless you and keep your journey,
Stan d for Jesus (my K Love nick name)

The Life Application Study Bible 3rd Edition, New International Version. Produced by Zondervan Grand Rapids MI and Tyndale House Publishers Carol Stream IL
The Gospel of the Kingdom, by George Eldon, Ladd
Moments of Joy, by Julie Hasling
Daily Power, by Paster Craig Groeschel
Seasons of Light in the Atchafalaya Basin, by Greg Guirard
The Discipleship Book, by Our Saviors Church, Doctor Scott Adams
In Jesus Name, by Doctor Scott Adams
Around the Year, by Emmett Fox
The Heart of a Servant, by Ron DiCinni
The Life of Paul Bible Study, Rose Publishing

My Utmost for His Highest, by Oswald Chambers
Mere Christianity, by C.S. Lewis
Knowledge of the Holy (Article), by A.W. Tozer
Dear Theophilus. Why did God create the world? (Article) by Michelle Pasley, MAT
The Cry of the Soul, by Doctor Dan B. Allender and Doctor Tremper Longman III
Race Lift, by Pastor Myron Guillory
Love is a Decision, by Gary Smalley with John Trent, PHD
The Five Love Languages, by Doctor Garry Chapman
Emotionally Healthy. Spiritually, by Peter Scazzero
The Emotionally Healthy Leader, by Peter Scazzero
Spiritual Leadership, by J Oswald Sanders
Evidence of Jesus? By, Josh McDowell and Sean McDowell
Evidence that Demands Verdict, by Josh McDowell and Sean McDowell
The Secret Power of Speaking God's Word, by Joyce Myer
Walking with God, by Doctor Charles F. Stanley
Jesus Calling: Enjoying Peace in His Presence, by Sarah Young
Living in Freedom Every day, Life Small Group Workbook
The Last Days According to Jesus, by R.C. Sproul
The Book of Revelation Made Easy, by Kenneth L. Gentry Jr.

ABOUT THE AUTHOR

I have only been a saved and deliberate Christian since March of 2017 at age 63. It was the live worship music that got my attention and launched me into a 6-year discovery journey of reading, researching, writing, Bible study, fellowship and Bible intensives. I had an epiphany of Jesus, our Savior, Teacher and Guiding Light and a revelation of the person God created me (and you)nto be. As boy and a young man, I was shy, socially awkward and so allowed bullies to define who I was. Eventually, I pushed back and pushed myself to take 2 college courses. I did not fail!! I moved on to achieve a master's degree in clinical social work and served God 28 years as a licensed clinical and forensic social worker for the Louisiana State Office of Mental Health. It is NEVER too late to discover the best version of yourself, come to know Jesus and discover the Christian Humanitarian in you… and a Mentality of Tranquility, walking with Jesus: The Prince of Peace.

Printed in the United States
by Baker & Taylor Publisher Services